STUDIES IN HISTORY, ECONOMICS, AND PUBLIC LAW

EDITED BY THE FACULTY OF POLITICAL SCIENCE
OF COLUMBIA UNIVERSITY

Number 282

DEMOCRACY AND FINANCE IN CHINA

A Study in the Development of Fiscal Systems and Ideals

DEMOCRACY AND FINANCE IN CHINA

A Study in the Development of
Fiscal Systems and Ideals

BY

KINN WEI SHAW

AMS PRESS
NEW YORK

COLUMBIA UNIVERSITY
STUDIES IN THE
SOCIAL SCIENCES
282

The series was formerly known as *Studies in History, Economics and Public Law.*

Reprinted with the permission of Columbia University Press
From the edition of 1926, New York
First AMS EDITION published 1970
Manufactured in the United States of America

Library of Congress Catalog Number: 73-127445
International Standard Book Number:
   Complete Set . . . 0-404-51000-0
   Number 282 0-404-51282-8

AMS PRESS, INC.
New York, N.Y. 10003

As a Token of Affection

To

MY BELOVED FATHER

WHO TAUGHT ME HOW TO STUDY CHINESE HISTORY AND PHILOSOPHY AND
HOW TO APPRECIATE THEM, WHO AWAKENED MY INTEREST IN THE
CONSTRUCTIVE ASPECTS OF PUBLIC FINANCE WHEN IN MY EARLIER
DAYS I WAS BEGUILED BY THE MODERN SCHOOLS OF RADICALISM
AND WHO HAS NEVER FAILED TO ENCOURAGE ME TO
DEVOTE MYSELF TO ACADEMIC LIFE AND TO CARRY
ON THE WORK IN MY ESPECIAL FIELD AS
THOROUGHLY AS POSSIBLE;

And to

MY BELOVED MOTHER

WHOSE IDEAL OF HIGH MORAL CHARACTER IS INSPIRING
AND WHOSE CARE OF MY FAMILY HAS ENABLED ME TO
DEVOTE ALL MY ATTENTION TO MY STUDIES
IN AMERICA

THIS BOOK IS RESPECTFULLY
DEDICATED

PREFACE

THE present volume of Dr. Shaw is interesting from several points of view. In the first place it shows us that there is indeed nothing new under the sun and that many of the ideas which we have considered as original with Western thinkers and statesmen are to be found in more or less developed form in their Eastern predecessors. It would indeed have been remarkable if the Chinese who at so early a period secured a primacy in philosophical and ethical discussion, should not have devoted much thought to certain problems, at least of fiscal obligation and fiscal practice. The economic and social conditions of China, it is true, are so entirely distinct from those of the Western world that economic speculation in that country necessarily assumed a different form from that found in Europe. The recital, however, by Dr. Shaw of the successive schools of thought on fiscal topics is impressive and cannot fail to be of value to all students.

In the second place, Dr. Shaw discloses a happy combination of the results of Eastern and Western training. Deeply versed in the classic lore of his own nation, he shows that he is able to put to good use the lessons of his American experience without being untrue to his own traditions. In this respect he is much like another of his countrymen, whose dissertation has been published in this series, Dr. Chen Huang-Chang, the author of " The Economic Principles of Confucius and His School."

Although it has been my good fortune to have had many able students of fiscal affairs among the young Chinese that throng the halls of Columbia, Dr. Shaw is perhaps the first who has assiduously devoted himself to a fiscal science which should be in harmony with the teachings of his own fore-bears. His dissertation ought therefore to be of consider-able value alike to the East and to the West. To his coun-trymen he brings the ripe fruits of an intimate acquaintance with all that is best in the modern fiscal science of Europe and America; to the Westerners he lifts for the first time the veil which has hitherto concealed the teachings and the motives that have guided fiscal theory and fiscal practice in China. For both of these reasons the book is warmly to be welcomed.

EDWIN R. A. SELIGMAN.

AUTHOR'S NOTE

THE study of Chinese finance may be approached from a theoretical or a practical point of view. In a theoretical study the sphere of inquiry may be limited to the fiscal philosophy of a particular school, or it may be broadened so as to include a comparative study of the various aspects of a number of schools. A practical study may trace the development of a system of taxation during a certain period or throughout the whole course of Chinese history, or it may concern itself with specific present-day problems such as tariff reform, land tax reform, and, as some political writers have suggested, a Chinese " Dawes Plan " for China.

In the following pages the author proposes, *first,* to discuss the probable influence which the various schools of ancient Chinese fiscal philosophy have exercised upon the fiscal psychology of the Chinese people; *second,* to interpret the sociological phases of Chinese finance by showing that any fundamental political or economic change has generally been accompanied, or followed, by a reform in the fiscal institutions, and to point out that any program for Chinese fiscal reconstruction today should give due consideration to sociological factors; and, *third,* to formulate a few principles of fiscal ethics in accordance with the ideal of true and progressive democracy and to present certain recommendations for their practical application in China. In other words, an attempt will be made in this study to develop a system of fiscal philosophy or ideology by harmonizing the fiscal ethics, the fiscal psychology and the fiscal sociology of the Chinese people, taking into account Chinese philosophy, history and present-day conditions.

Grateful acknowledgment is made to Professors John Dewey, R. M. Haig, Paul Pelliot, and Lewis Hodous, of Columbia University, and Professor J. H. Hollander of the Johns Hopkins University, for their invaluable advice and assistance in the preparation of this work, and to Mrs. C. A. Stewart, secretary to Professor Seligman, and Miss Mary R. Boulger, of the Rockefeller Foundation, for their literary criticism.

A word of gratitude is due the friends of the author, especially Dr. P. W. Kuo, director of the China Institute in America, New York City; Professor Y. C. Ma, of Peking National University; Professor C. T. Tsai, of the Tsing Hua College, Peking; Dr. C. S. Li, of the Fuh Tan University, Shanghai; Professor T. D. Woo, of the Government College of Law and Political Sciences, Hangchow; Professor W. W. Wong, now editor-in-chief of the Commercial Press, Shanghai; Mr. T. Sheng, director of the Ministry of Finance Bureau of Markets, Shanghai; Mr. S. M. Chang, of the Ministry of Foreign Affairs, Peking; Messrs. N. T. Chao, C. T. Liu, and Milton C. Lee, of Columbia University; and his brother, Miachen S. Shaw, of the University of Washington, for their sincere encouragement and valuable suggestions.

The author owes his greatest obligation to Professor Edwin R. A. Seligman, McVickar Professor of Political Economy in Columbia University, under whose inspiring guidance, constant encouragement, sound teaching, and constructive criticism this monograph has attained its present form.

KINN WEI SHAW

COLUMBIA UNIVERSITY, MAY, 1926.

CONTENTS

CONTENTS

APPENDIX I

APPENDIX II

PART ONE

Introduction

THE EARLY DEVELOPMENT OF FISCAL STUDY IN CHINA

Public Finance is a new science in China today. However, it is a subject that has attracted the attention of political philosophers and historical writers from antiquity. The first authentic record of the ancient tax system, handed down in a compilation of Confucius under the title, "Tribute System of Yü," [1] dates back almost four thousand years. In the "Chou Kuan," [2] a code of the constitutional and administrative laws of the Chou dynasty, a period extending from 1122 B. C. to 256 B. C. and generally known as the Golden Age of the ancient Middle Kingdom, we find elaborate provisions for governmental budgetary and accounting procedure. When we turn to the writings on political history, we discover that such subjects as "Government Fiscal Policies" [3] and "Status of National Economy" [4] have received the attention of historians since the days of Ssŭ-ma Ch'ien, the great Chinese historian of the second century B. C. Moreover, if we undertake to trace the historical development of the land tax, of taxes on commodities or of the government monopolies of salt and iron, we find that a

[1] *Chinese Classics*, vol. iii, pt. iii, pp. 92-151.

[2] Sometimes translated "The Official System of Chou," or "State Regulations of the Chou Dynasty." In the present monograph, this great document is called "The Constitution of the Chou dynasty."

[3] *Historical Record*, ch. 86.

[4] *Ibid.*, ch. 152.

wealth of material is available on these subjects. It may be said, therefore, that Chinese finance in its historical aspect offers a wide field for scientific research.

If we approach the subject from the angle of theoretical analysis, we find that the course of Chinese fiscal history has been marked throughout by controversy between principle and expediency, or, as we may say, between idealism and empiricism. The period in which this controversy reached its highest point was the latter part of the Chou dynasty (770-249 B. C), which really constituted the stage of transition from feudal to imperial finance. During this period the country fell into a state of such disorder that the existing laws and regulations no longer sufficed to maintain the old fiscal régime. The central government was weak. The feudal chiefs of the stronger states fought against each other for political and military supremacy. More than this, the noble classes abused their powers to an alarming extent; and lawlessness, rather than law, became the rule of the day. Taxation grew more and more burdensome, and the requirements of military service unbearable.

Aroused by such evils, a number of political thinkers undertook to discover some means of fiscal reconstruction and economic salvation. These reformers included Lao Tzǔ, Confucius, Mo Ti, a group calling themselves the Agriculturalists, and a group known as the Jurists. Lao Tzǔ, Mo Ti, and the Agriculturalists formulated fiscal programs embodying certain idealistic principles; the Jurists advocated practical expediency in national fiscal policies rather than the pursuit of some ideal of social justice; while the school of Confucius usually held a golden mean between the two extremes. Let us examine briefly the fiscal principles and policies of these several philosophers and their schools.

School of Lao Tzŭ

The fundamental doctrine of the school founded by Lao Tzŭ,[1] a free-thinker of the latter part of the Chou dynasty, was natural liberty of the individual. On nearly every page of his immortal work, *Tao Teh King,* or *Nature versus Nurture,* he bears witness to his belief in the principle of non-interference on the part of the government. His motto, " Government, do nothing!", meaning thereby that the less the government does for its people, the more they will be able to care for themselves, had in reality the same implication as that of the French Physiocracy, " laissez faire, laissez passer." On the basis of this principle, he attacked the paternalistic government of his time as the main source of political and social evils. He maintained that the best government is the least government, that is, one in which there is minimum interference by the government and maximum autonomy for the governed. He said:

As restrictions and prohibitions are multiplied in the state, the people grow poorer and poorer; the greater the number of laws and enactments, the more thieves and robbers there will be. So long as the ruler practices non-interference, the people will work out their own salvation; so long as he preserves an attitude of detachment, they will develop in the right direction; if only he refrains from undue expansion of governmental functions, they will of their own accord become industrious and prosperous; and if only he frees himself from avarice and pretension, they will naturally follow his example and return to simplicity and honesty.[2]

From this declaration we see that Lao Tzŭ's government of non-interference is essentially similar to that which the Physiocrats called the " ordre naturel ".

[1] Lived about six or five centuries B. C.
[2] *Tao Teh King,* ch. 57.

The political utopia of Lao Tzŭ was a collection of small self-governing communities which had entirely freed themselves from unnecessary and vexatious governmental restrictions. These communities may be designated as village states in distinction to the city states which existed in ancient Greece. In one of the concluding chapters of his *Tao Teh King,* Lao Tzŭ described the ideal state in the following way:

> In a small state with few inhabitants, let there be aldermen and mayors who possess power over the people but who never use it. Let the people hold their native region in high regard and not seek to leave it for a distant locality or state at the risk of safety. Although they have ships and carriages, let them not seek to journey abroad therein. Although they have armor and weapons, let them find no occasion to display them. Let them return to the old custom of using knotted cords in place of writing. Let them provide themselves with satisfying food, beautiful clothing, tranquil homes, and happy environment. Then shall residents of neighboring communities, dwelling within sight of one another's homes and within hearing of the clamor of one another's cocks and dogs, grow old and die without having exchanged visits.[1]

Thus it would appear that Lao Tzŭ disapproved not only of government interference, but also of territorial aggrandizement, military aspirations, and imperialistic economic policies, and that he advocated an economic civilization which was agricultural rather than industrial and commercial. For these reasons, his school may be called the Physiocratic school of ancient Chinese economic philosophy.

Lao Tzŭ held that, as a natural result of the application of the principle of government by non-interference and government in the form of a loose confederacy, which was in

---

[1] *Tao Teh King,* ch. 80.

reality a composite body of numerous village republics, government functions would be reduced to a minimum, and the burden of taxation would be lightened. In his opinion, the safeguards against the exploitation of a people by its government were limitation of bureaucratic activities and strict observance of the rule of governmental frugality. The first of these safeguards was a problem of practical government; the second, one of practical economy. Both were considered by him as prerequisite to a moderate system of taxation. " In running a government," he said, " liberality without frugality rings the death-knell of the nation." [1] He also declared, " The people starve because those in authority devour too many taxes." [2]

In connection with Lao Tzŭ's insistence on the necessity of governmental economy, it is of interest to recall the words of Frederick the Great, who believed that onerous taxation, levied without regard to the exhaustion of the source of national revenue, would inevitably bring a nation to bankruptcy. The statement as quoted by Roscher in his *Finanzwissenschaft* reads : " The state will bankrupt itself if it adopts the policy of saying, ' I need so much; raise the money,' rather than, ' I have so much, and can therefore spend so much.' " [3] Both of these philosopher-statesmen believed not only that the people should be taxed in accordance with their ability to pay, but that they should be freed from oppressive taxation so that they might have a reserve or surplus ability to pay.

The politico-economic principles of Lao Tzŭ have occupied a unique position in the development of Chinese fiscal

[1] *Tao Teh King*, ch. 67.

[2] *Ibid.*, ch. 75.

[3] Section 109. See also Bullock, *Selected Readings in Public Finance,* New York, 1924, 3rd ed., p. 21.

thought. He impressed upon the consciousness of his race for all time a distaste for paternalistic government and a belief in the importance of village autonomy. Although the school of Confucius has again and again attained ascendency in political and educational fields, the fiscal philosophy of Lao Tzŭ has, as a rule, remained that of the Chinese statesmen. The most successful economist-rulers in the fiscal history of China, especially those of the periods of reconstruction after the turmoil of great revolutions, have for the most part been the faithful students of this remarkable philosopher. Foremost among these were Emperor Wên of the Former Han dynasty and Emperor Wên of the Sui dynasty, both of whom brought about an extraordinary economic prosperity by carrying out the policy of light taxation and rigid economy in government expenditures.[1]

However, the fiscal philosophy of Lao Tzŭ is not without its shortcomings. It is indisputable that when the people at large need immediate relief from a burden of excessive taxation, rigid economy in public expenditures and a reduction of the rate of taxation are the necessary, and usually helpful, measures for a government to take. Nevertheless it does not follow that relief from excessive taxation will solve once and for all the problem of fiscal rehabilitation and reconstruction. The Chinese economist-rulers and other financiers have usually contented themselves with the accomplishment of this first step and have not attempted to go further. This is the outstanding defect of Chinese fiscal conservatism, and its development must to a large extent be ascribed to the school of Lao Tzŭ.

Two other schools of the five which we have under consideration held nearly the same view as that of Lao Tzŭ.

[1] *Infra.*

These were the school of Mo Ti and that of the Agriculturalists. We shall therefore consider next the fiscal philosophy of these two.

School of Mo Ti

The crux of the fiscal philosophy of Mo Ti [1] was economy. He held that in regulating governmental expenditures, the first question to be asked is, " Is their increase necessary or can public affairs be managed without such increment?" He believed that all government disbursements should be carefully scrutinized and every unnecessary or wasteful item eliminated.[2] He also maintained that every increase of government expenditure and service without proportional increase of public benefit should be avoided if the government is to be wisely and efficiently conducted.[3]

But his contribution to the development of Chinese fiscal thought is not simply this emphasis on the need of governmental frugality. He pointed out that the economical administration of a state is made possible only by the elimination of expenses for war or for the preparation for war. He attacked militarism and its foster parents, short-sighted patriotism and one-sided nationalism, upon humanitarian as well as economic grounds. Indeed Mo Ti has sometimes been called the Jesus Christ of China, because of his great spirit of sacrifice, and his doctrine of universal love and universal peace, two of his celebrated " ten commandments." [4]

To him peace was an international problem; but realizing that international peace could be more effectively maintained by the practice of cooperative defence among the smaller and weaker nations than by reliance upon the good will of the

[1] Born 468 or 459 B. C.
[2] *The Works of Mo Tzŭ*, ch. xx.
[3] *Ibid.*, chs. vi and xxi.
[4] *Ibid.*, ch. 49.

stronger states towards the weaker ones, Mo Ti said: "For the sake of mutual protection, an agreement must be reached by the small nations that whenever one of them is in danger of invasion, the others, especially neighboring states, will come to the rescue as soon as the situation permits."[1]

This indicates that the principle he advocated is better designated as "defensism" than as "pacifism." That he did not favor extreme pacifism is evident from the fact that in his collected works, 22 out of 71 chapters deal with the tactics of defense.[2] But he held that if states continued to regard war as the only means of settling international differences, no national fiscal policy worthy of the name of constructive finance would be possible. He said: "Notwithstanding that some four or five nations might derive much profit from aggressive wars in so far as spoils or other material gains are concerned, that would not make war a practical, expedient policy from the standpoint of the world as a whole."[3] This would indicate a belief that after all war is an evil, and can never be a legitimate aim, whether considered from a social, a political, or an economic standpoint.

School of the Agriculturalists

Of the five leading schools of ancient Chinese political philosophy, the one whose doctrines are least deliberately expounded is the school of Agriculturalists, founded by Hsü Hsing, who is sometimes styled the Tolstoi of ancient China. No single book has ever been written on the political and economic theories of this school, and the material on which to base our discussion can only be collected from the works

---

[1] *The Works of Mo Tzŭ*, ch. 52.

[2] Twelve of these chapters on defence are still in our possession, viz., chs. 50, 52, 53, 56, 58, 61, 62, 63, 68, 69, 70 and 71.

[3] *The Works of Mo Tzŭ*, chs. xviii and xix.

of Mencius, the great Confucian, a contemporary of Hsü Hsing and a most influential opponent of his school.

It is a well-recognized fact that the Chinese people are, in a certain sense, inherently practical anarchists. Although it was the school of Lao Tzŭ that was most influential in moulding this political attitude and tradition, the school of Agriculturalists played an important part in keeping alive the sacred fires of the faith. Hsü Hsing, like Lao Tzŭ, advocated the village state, but he went a step further in that he thought the ruler of such a state should engage in the same business as did the mass of people over whom he ruled, that is, the pursuit of agriculture. He counseled following the teachings of Shên Nung, the celebrated father of Chinese husbandry, ruler of the Middle Kingdom about the 28th century B. C., according to whom every sovereign should be a farmer, cultivating the land equally and together with his people, and reaping only the fruits of his labor; preparing his meals morning and evening, and at the same time carrying on the affairs of government.[1] Following the example of the ruler himself, those subordinate to his authority should also live from hand to mouth.

It is evident, therefore, that what Hsü Hsing considered the necessary occupations were those which more or less related to the production and exchange of the necessities of life, and that the keynote of his doctrine was the agriculturalization of society. He advocated a social order centered in cooperative farming as against competitive commercial enterprise, in rural self-government as against bureaucratic autocracy, and in the régime of labor as against that of capital. He approved the allotment of public lands for cooperative cultivation and held that both the governing and the governed should be self-supporting by their own labor so that there would be no further need for taxation. He

[1] *Chinese Classics,* vol. ii, p. 246.

said: "The ideal ruler keeps no granaries, no treasuries and no arsenals. If he has such things as these, he is oppressing the people for his own support."[1] This statement shows that Hsü Hsing had in mind a fiscal system without taxation, and a fiscal policy of an extremely pacifistic and mutualistic nature. His ideal, however, was more a political utopia than a fiscal possibility. Just as the equalization and standardization of working and living conditions were prerequisites to the establishment of his non-capitalistic régime, so universal pacifism and complete disarmament were the antecedent conditions necessary to the realization of his non-militaristic fiscal ideal.

In justice to the school of Hsü Hsing, which has long been known as the school of anarchists, its negation of governmental interference should not be interpreted as a negation of the existence of government such as was advanced by Pan Ku, a great Confucian historian of the Latter Han dynasty, and his followers.[2] The Agriculturalists avowed themselves to be practical workers, rather than propagandist doctrinaires. The teachings of the latter were decried by them as unproductive and misleading.

The Agriculturalists' neglect of propaganda and the misinterpretation of their teachings by the orthodox Confucians are the causes to which we may attribute the lack of academic interest in their doctrines and the exclusion of these from the field of political and social discussion after the school of Confucius had established itself as the Chinese national orthodox socio-political religion. Furthermore, after the abolition of the public land system, the allotment of fields for cooperative cultivation, which was practically essential to the successful operation of the economic program of the Agriculturalists, was no longer possible.

[1] *Chinese Classics,* vol. ii, p. 247.
[2] *History of Han,* ch. xxx, folio 10.

All three of the schools with which we have so far dealt preached the doctrine of minimum governmental interference. Their fiscal discussions were concerned more with the limitation and regulation of government expenditure than with the reform of the revenue system. We shall now pass on to a consideration of the fiscal philosophy of the school of the Jurists, which favored maximum state control and formulated its fiscal policies with a view to the realization of substantial government revenue and the carrying out of its nationalistic and imperialistic political programs.

School of the Jurists

The Teachings of Kuan Tzŭ.—The best exposition of the fiscal philosophy of the Jurists is given in the *Works of Kuan Tzŭ*,[1] prime minister of the state of Ch'i in the seventh century B. C., renowned for the success of his fiscal administration. The basic principle of Kuan Tzŭ's program for fiscal reconstruction was indirect taxation through government monopoly of certain necessities of daily consumption, coupled with state control of the prices of these commodities. His policy was to constitute the state a capitalist, an entrepreneur, and the sole regulator of the economic life of society. It has been well pointed out by Liang Chi-ch'ao, a recognized authority on Chinese political and economic philosophy, that the policy of financing a government without resort to the exaction of direct taxation, but relying chiefly on the revenues of government monopoly, as advocated and practised by Kuan Tzŭ, may be properly called the system of " the single consumption tax." [2]

---

[1] This work was not written entirely by Kuan Tzŭ himself, but was compiled after his death by his followers, who made certain interpolations of their own.

[2] Liang Chi-ch'ao, " On the Causes of the Neglect of Fiscal Study in China," *Ta Chun Hua Monthly*, Shanghai, Feb. 20, 1914, vol. i, pp. 1-6.

Kuan Tzŭ maintained that most taxes have their evil results, to wit, the house tax discourages the building of new dwellings and brings about the deterioration of the old ones by consuming the funds that should be devoted to improvements. The tax on cattle and other domesticated animals impairs the industry of stock raising; that on acreage of land, the industry of agriculture. If a poll tax were levied according to the number of adults, the happiness of home life would be injured and the people's regard for their government would be lessened. If a tax were to be imposed according to the number of families, then the independent families of small means would be compelled to become dependents of the rich ones.[1] "All these," he said, " are exactions by compulsion which would not be approved by any wise statesman. What such a one would do is to tax the people without letting them know that they were being taxed." [2] He advocated, therefore, that revenue be secured through the establishment of government monopolies of salt and iron and the nationalization of forests and mines.

In support of his monopolistic policies he said:

. . . In a family of ten persons, there are ten consumers of salt; in a family of a hundred persons, there are hundred consumers of salt. On an average, each male adult takes about five and a half *sheng*[3] of this commodity each month; each female adult, three and a half *sheng*; and minors, two and a half *sheng*. Now, if salt is taxed at the rate of one-half of a *cash*[4] per *sheng*, the revenue derived from 100 *sheng* will be fifty *cash*; if the rate is fixed at one or two *cash* a *sheng*, the revenue from 100 *sheng* will be 100 or 200 *cash* respectively.

[1] *The Works of Kuan Tzŭ*, vol. xxii, ch. 73, folio 4.

[2] *Ibid.*, folio 3.

[3] *A sheng* is about 1.095 quarts.

[4] A *cash* is one-thousandth of a Chinese dollar.

If 1,000 *sheng* are consumed, and the tax rate is two *cash* a *sheng*, the revenue will be 2,000 *cash*; if 10,000, or 100,000, or 1,000,000 *sheng* are consumed, the revenue resulting will be 20,000, or 200,000, or 2,000,000 *cash* respectively. On an average, the daily revenue from the salt tax of a nation with a population of 10,000,000, can be estimated at 2,000,000 *cash*. This will make a revenue of 20,000,000 *cash* for every ten days; and one of 60,000,000 *cash* per month. If, on the other hand, a poll tax were levied at the rate of ten *cash* per month for every three persons,[1] and taxable adults of the whole population are numbered at 9,000,000, the monthly revenue would amount to only 30,000,000 *cash*, while the people at large would be greatly vexed and troubled. For the salt, which they have to use every day, however, they pay willingly. As a consequence the government can, through the salt tax, raise with ease double the revenue to be derived through the exaction of a poll tax. . . . [2]

. . . According to the estimate made by the " iron officers," every woman possesses a needle and a knife; every farmer, a plow, a harrow and a scythe; and every carpenter, an axe, a saw, a hammer and a chisel. If, then, the steel for the manufacture of the needle is taxed according to one-tenth of the weight of a needle or, to use the money equivalent, one *cash* for each needle, the revenue derived from the sale of thirty needles will amount to that derived from the annual poll-tax paid by an adult. If knives are taxed on the basis of their raw material or at the rate of six *cash* each, the sale of five knives will bring in the equivalent of an annual poll-tax. If plows are taxed according to the amount of iron used in their manufacture, or at the rate of ten *cash* each, the revenue brought in by the sale of three plows will also be equal to that from an annual poll-tax.[3]

---

[1] Compare this with the interpretation suggested by Liang Chi-ch'ao in his work *Kuan Tzŭ, the Statesman*, p. 101.

[2] *The Works of Kuan Tzŭ*, vol. xxii, ch. 72, folios 1 and 2.

[3] *Ibid.*, vol. xxii, ch. 72, folio 2.

Thus Kuan Tzŭ's policy of the monopoly of iron centred simply in the control of the raw material, not in the manufacture of iron wares by the government itself. The latter policy he once criticized on the grounds that if the government compelled the convicts or slaves to work in iron foundries, they would flee as soon as opportunity offered; and if the common people were forced to work in these places, they would hate their government to the extreme, and would refuse to fight for it when foreign invasion or other emergency occurred. He held that the wisest procedure for the government was to control the supply of raw iron and so to regulate its price that 30 per cent of the price would go to the government treasury, while the other 70 per cent would be the compensation for those engaged in the iron industry.[1] Under this policy every self-supporting man and woman would pay his or her tax in the form of prices, without reluctance and without possibility of evasion.[2]

Kuan Tzŭ was once asked by Huan Kung, the duke of the state of Ch'i, " What shall a state do if it possesses no special natural resources such as salt and iron?" He replied, " Employ the natural resources of other states by adopting a modified system of government monopoly, or the system of the monopoly of foreign imports. For instance, if the price of sale is fifteen *cash* per 100 *sheng* in the state where it is produced, let the government of the state which is without this resource buy up a supply of it and sell it again at the price of 100 *cash* per 100 *sheng*." [3] He called this the policy of employing the natural resources of other states as those of one's own state, and the citizens of other state as one's own people.[4] This policy of imperialistic

[1] *The Works of Kuan Tzŭ,* vol. xxiv, ch. 81, folios 1 and 2.

[2] *Ibid.,* vol. xxiv, ch. 81, folios 1 and 2.

[3] *Ibid.*

[4] *Ibid.* See also vol. xxiii, ch. 77, folio 2.

economic exploitation contributed much to his success in raising the state of Ch'i to an economic and political supremacy, but it was much deplored by the Confucians, who considered it in direct opposition to their doctrines of economic universalism, the mainstays of which were state ownership of land and unrestrained international free trade.

Kuan Tzŭ succeeded in effecting the nationalization of both mines and forestry. After accomplishing this he graded the forest woods into three classes according to their quality, viz., (i) wood for temporary use, as fire wood, (ii) wood for permanent use, such as building materials, and (iii) wood of extreme permanency, as for burial caskets. The lowest price was charged for the first kind; a higher one for the second; and the highest one for the third.[1] Thereby he was able to abolish the tax on the rent of forest land, because he collected an equal, and sometimes even a greater, revenue in the form of prices paid for fuel or other materials. He held that by such an arrangement the burden of taxation might be more equitably distributed, because it left the people free to buy and to pay as much as they could afford.[2]

With regard to the nationalization of mines, Kuan Tzŭ said: " Where there is ochre on the surface of ground, there is iron below; where there is zinc, cinnabar, lodestone, or galenic stone on the surface, there is silver, gold, copper, zinc, or tin respectively underneath." All the mountainous districts which bore such signs on the surface of their land were nationalized, and strict punishments were imposed by the government upon those who worked the mines without proper authorization.[3]

---

[1] *The Works of Kuan Tzŭ*, vol. xxii, ch. 74, folio 6.

[2] *Ibid.*, folio 7. This policy of public ownership of forestry sharply differentiated the school of Jurists from that of Confucius, because the latter's advocacy of the conservation of forestry by state regulations, but not by state ownership, was based essentially on social, not fiscal, grounds.

[3] *Ibid.*, vol. xxiii, ch. 77, folio 1.

These measures prepared the way for Kuan Tzŭ's program of fiscal centralism, of which the most important feature was the government control of the supply of money and of the prices of commodities.[1] The nationalization of mines was a means toward this end in that it put the supply of gold and other money materials at the disposal of the government. At that time a triple monetary standard was maintained, that is, the pearl for the highest denomination, the gold coin for the intermediate, and the copper coin for the lowest. But of these the gold currency was the most important one, and the control of its supply was considered by Kuan Tzŭ as the sole method of regulating the money market.[2]

A second step taken by Kuan Tzŭ for the control of prices was the adjustment of the volume of the various forms of currency to the needs of society. He ascertained the demand for currency by dividing the state into a number of monetary districts, the smallest of which were districts of six Chinese square miles each, and taking into account the following factors, (i) the quality or productivity of the land within that district, (ii) the amount of grain produced, (iii) the price of the grain, (iv) the amount of money in circulation, and (v) the amount of currency especially needed for the grain trade.[3]

He also investigated the relation between the price of grain and that of other commodities. He held that not only

---

[1] Of the 86 chapters of Kuan Tzŭ's work, 19 are devoted to the subject "Heaviness or Lightness," the former denoting demand in excess of supply, the latter supply in excess of demand. Of these 19 chapters, 16 are still available, viz., chs. 68 to 81, and chs. 83 to 85. Chapter 72, which deals with the policy of salt and iron monopolies, and chapter 73 dealing with the government control of supply and demand, are especially deserving of intensive study.

[2] *The Works of Kuan Tzŭ*, vol. xxiv, ch. 81, folio 1.

[3] *Ibid.*, vol. xxii, ch. 76, folios 11 and 12.

the power of coinage and the control of the supply of money should be centralized in the national government, but also the control of grain supply; otherwise, the poorer classes of the people would be at the mercy of " grain ringers." He maintained that the price of grain was the most representative of all the commodity prices. If its price rose, owing to the shortage of supply and the increasing demand of the market, the prices of other commodities would fall. If its price should fall, owing to the abundance of supply and the falling off of demand, the prices of other commodities would rise.[1] The explanation of this is that at that time the barter system was still in existence, and grain was not only an objective in the bartering, but also a medium of exchange in the rural communities. Therefore the rise and fall of the price of this principal merchandise in the market served as a fair index of the general rise or fall of the prices of other commodities. These various recommendations serve to show that Kuan Tzŭ was both a financier and an economist. He understood the nature of money so well that he did not consider it the only form of wealth, but merely one of its various forms.[2]

In the preceding paragraphs we have been concerned with Kuan Tzŭ's measures for raising national revenues. Now, let us proceed to consider how he spent the money so raised, because the aim of the statesman, as Bastable has well said, is not simply to distribute loss and reduce it to a minimum, but rather to procure the maximum of advantage to the community, and to so balance expenditure and revenue as to attain that result.[3] The following is a summary of the principles in accordance with which Kuan Tzŭ regulated the expenditures of his government.

[1] *The Works of Kuan Tzŭ*, vol. xxii, ch. 76, folio 12.

[2] *Ibid.*, vol. xxii, ch. 73, folio 1.

[3] Bastable, C. F., *Public Finance*, 3rd ed., 1903, p. 7.

Principles for the Regulation of Governmental Expenditures. — The principles of governmental expenditure which Kuan Tzŭ laid down were nine in number.[1]   To wit:

I. *Expenditure for the Care of the Aged.*—The officer in charge of the administration for the care of the aged was delegated to look after the living conditions of those under his care, exempting the sons of the aged from military and other personal services for the public, one son to be exempted when the man reached the age of seventy, two when he reached the age of eighty, and all when he reached ninety.   The burial expenses of the aged were partly defrayed by the government.

II. *Expenditure for the Care of Children.*—The officer in charge of this branch of the administration was empowered to exempt the mother of three children from paying any exaction of cloth and hemp; if she had four children, the whole family were to be exempt from military and other personal service. If she had five children, a public nurse was to be assigned to take care of the younger two, who were to be supported by the government until they were able to support themselves.

III. *Expenditure for the Welfare of Orphans.*—The officer in charge of the bureau for the welfare of the orphans was responsible for their living conditions, exempting the family which was interested in bringing up one, two, or three children, from paying the personal-service tax of one, two, or all members of that family respectively.

IV. *Expenditure for the Care of the Disabled.*—Every deaf, blind, lame, or otherwise deformed or disabled man, who could not take care of himself was to be supported by the government and to receive free medical treatment at the government hospital.

V. *Expenditure for the Care of Widows and Widowers.*— The officer of this service was called a public matchmaker.   He went between the widow and widower and advised them to marry when he saw fit.   If they came to an agreement and got married, they were given a house in which to make their home and an

[1] *The Works of Kuan Tzŭ*, vol. xviii, ch. 54, folio 1.

allotment of land for cultivation. They were not taxed until three years after their marriage.

VI. *Expenditure for the Care of the Sick.*—The officer in charge of this division of the administration was a visiting physician-in-chief. Every visiting physician was delegated to visit regularly the homes in the district assigned to him in order that he might see whether any people were sick. If the patient was a scholar and above the age of ninety, he was to be called upon and examined by the physician every day; if he was above eighty, once every two days; above seventy, once every three days. If he was seriously sick, the visiting physician was required to report the fact to the prince in order that the latter might pay a visit to the patient and give him his personal consolation.

VI. *Expenditure for the Care of the Homeless and Travellers in Distress.*—Communities in which homeless persons or needy travellers were found were required to report these cases to the authorities. The residents of the locality reporting such cases were to be rewarded. Failure to make such reports was a punishable offense.

VIII. *Expenditure for Special Relief.*—If there occurred a famine or plague, the stores in the governmental granaries were to be distributed for relief.

IX. *Expenditure for Memorials to Those who Sacrificed Their Lives for the State.*—The relatives or friends of a man who died in war or in other public services were to be given a sum of money for the erection of a hall in memory of the distinguished service of their kinsman.

These nine kinds of public expenditure were called by Kuan Tzŭ the "nine items of welfare administration". He put them into practice shortly after accepting the premiership of the state of Ch'i.

Kuan Tzŭ reduced military expenditures to a minimum by adopting a system which he called "military preparedness in the form of a well-disciplined militia."[1] On the

[1] *The Works of Kuan Tzŭ*, vol. viii, ch. xx, folios 5 and 6.

other hand, he spent rather lavishly for the furtherance of
international good-will. At one time, two-thirds of the annual expenditure of the state was for this purpose.[1] This
is one of the reasons why the various princes of the time
were brought together under his leadership in international
conference on nine occasions.[2]

Fiscal Doctrines of Li Kuei and Shang Yang.—Two Jurists whose theories flourished during the latter part of the
Chou dynasty and who are deserving of special mention
were Li Kuei [3] (424-378 B. C.) and Shang Yang (360-338
B. C.), prime ministers of the state of Wei and the state of
Ch'in respectively. Li Kuei was particularly noted for elab-
orating a system of government control of the price level
of grain, and for his principle of maximum utilization of
the productive power of land. He declared:

Within an area one hundred *li,* or Chinese miles, square, there
are nine million *mou* or Chinese acres. Excluding the moun-
tains, marshes and city residences, one-third of this amount,
there are six million *mou* of arable land. If the people cultivate
their fields intensively, each acre can be made to yield three
additional *tou,* or Chinese pecks, of grain. Therefore, within
an area only one hundred *li* square, an increased yield of one
million eight hundred thousand *shih* or Chinese bushels can be
obtained.[4]

Having stimulated an interest in increased production

[1] *Ibid.,* vol. viii, ch. ix, folio 1.

[2] *Confucian Analects,* bk. xiv, ch. xvii, sec. ii.

[3] Dr. Chen Huan-chang has contended that the correct name was Li Ko
and that Li Ko was a Confucian. But, according to the *History of Han,*
Li Kuei should be accredited as the founder of the school of Jurists and
Li Ko, the Confucian, was a different person, although the latter was also
the prime minister of Wei. This view has been more generally held.
See *History of Han,* ch. xxx, folios 5-8.

[4] *History of Han,* ch. xxiv, folio 1.

Li Kuei turned his attention to the justice of distribution. He maintained that if the price of grain were too high, consumers would be injured, and would therefore emigrate to other countries. If it were too low, the farmers would suffer and the nation as a whole would remain in a state of poverty. He declared that what a government should do for the amelioration of such conditions or for the prevention of such evils is to place under government control the price level of grain and keep it as normal as possible. In other words, the government should buy up the excess supply of grain in good years when its price was below the normal, in order to meet the demand in bad years when prices rose far above the normal level.[1] In advocating this measure he was, as a matter of fact, merely adopting one of the policies which Kuan Tzŭ had successfully put into effect a few centuries before. His only real contribution was that he laid more stress on the development of agriculture and worked out the plan for government control of grain prices more fully and elaborately.[2]

Shang Yang, who was one of the most iron-handed statesmen China has ever produced, also believed that the salvation of the country lay in the maximum development of its agricultural facilities.[3] He considered that this development was hampered by the system of public ownership of land then in effect. He, therefore, advocated the legal recognition of private property and held that people should be allowed to own as much land as they pleased. Although this policy was vehemently condemned by the orthodox Confucians as undermining the economic structure of the whole

---

[1] *History of Han*, ch. xxiv, folios 1-2.

[2] For the details of the operation of Li Kuei's policy, consult Chen Huan-chang, *Economic Principles of Confucius and His School*, on Li Ko, pp. 569-570.

[3] *Book of the Lord of Shang, passim.*

empire, the necessity for the change was recognized by the people, and Shang Yang succeeded in bringing the public land system to an end.

The Strength and Weaknesses of the School of Jurists.— We have seen that Kuan Tzŭ, Li Kuei, and Shang Yang, the leading Jurists of ancient China, were all practical statesmen, and that they were believers in fiscal empiricism rather than in fiscal idealism. They laid down no definite program for their followers; their only creed was that a change of fiscal institutions should be made as soon as political and economic changes demanded it. In other words, they had no principle other than that of practical expediency.

This principle of fiscal expediency had, of course, its merits; but it had also certain defects. It led the average statesman to subordinate the interests of the people to those of the government, and not uncommonly placed the public purse at the disposal of a despot or a worthless king. This explains why the school of Jurists has too often lost its hold on Chinese fiscal thought. Moreover, the system of indirect taxation by means of monopolistic policies, as practised by Kuan Tzŭ and followed by the financiers of later periods, has resulted in an excessive burden on the mass of the Chinese people. In spite of these facts, Kuan Tzŭ and his followers were unrivaled in their specific and detailed study of fiscal problems during their period; and their keen insight into the needs of the time has well proved the serviceableness of practical fiscal experts in the solution of practical fiscal problems.

The Need of Balance between Fiscal Idealism and Fiscal Empiricism.—Thus far we have dealt with the two extremes of Chinese fiscal thought. The schools of Lao Tzŭ, Mo Ti, and the Agriculturalists stood for fiscal idealism in one way or another, while the fiscal dogma of the Jurists was nothing but practical expediency. Let us now turn to a study of the theories of a school which held an eclectic viewpoint, striking a balance between fiscal idealism and fiscal empiricism, that is, the school of Confucius.

School of Confucius

The fiscal principles laid down by Confucius and his school were of a threefold nature, dealing with revenue, expenditure, and the relation between revenue and expenditure. Let us examine these principles in detail.

Principles Relating to Revenue.—The school of Confucius stood, first of all, for the principle of fiscal justice. In the last chapter of the *Great Learning* we read: " In a state, pecuniary gain is not to be considered prosperity, but prosperity will be found in fiscal justice." [1] In the *Yi King* or *Book of Changes,* Confucius defined political justice as consisting of three elements, viz., proper regulation of social wealth and public finance (economic), honesty in government and care in the education of the people (ethical), and legitimate enforcement of the prohibitions against wrongdoing (legal).[2] It is noteworthy that in this enumeration fiscal justice occupied the foremost place. This principle the early Confucians sought to apply in the following ways: First, they supported state ownership of land with its equitable allotment for cultivation.[3] Second, they advocated a system of taxation limited to a proportional tax at the rate of one-tenth or, if necessary, one-ninth of the produce of the land.[4] Third, they held that the numerous taxes on

---

[1] *Chinese Classics,* vol. i, pp. 380-381.

[2] *Ying King,* appendix iii, sec. ii, ch. x.

[3] For a detailed analysis of this system, see *infra,* pp. 49-60.

[4] *Confucian Analects,* bk. vii, ch. ix, sec. i. See also *The Works of Mencius,* bk. i, pt. i, ch. iii, sec. xv.

necessities of life should be abolished, that a policy of free trade should be adopted for the furtherance of international commerce, and that only inspection offices should be established at the ports of entry along the national boundaries.[1] Fourth, they maintained that certain exemptions from taxation or personal service should be allowed on the ground of social expediency, e. g., the exemption of the aged and of minors from the exaction of corvées.[2] Fifth, they gave serious consideration to the convenience of the people, insisting, for example, that they should not be called from their husbandry in busy seasons for military expeditions or other public services.[3]

Principles regulating Governmental Expenditures.—Legitimate economy and constructive humanitarianism were the principles which the Confucians sought to follow in government expenditure. Confucius considered economy as one of the essentials of good government.[4] By this, however, he did not mean that the salaries of officials should be niggardly, for he held that ample remuneration for government employees constitutes an effective encouragement to faithful service.[5] His conception of economy is best illustrated by this passage from the *Book of Changes:* " If the expenditures of a government are regulated according to the principle of legitimate economy, no public money will be wasted and the people will suffer no unjust and excessive taxation or other exactions." [6] The constructive humanitarian policies advocated by the school of Confucius may be summarized as

---

[1] *The Works of Mencius,* bk. i, pt. ii, ch. v, sec. iii, and bk. iii, pt. i, ch. iii, sec. xv.

[2] *Cf. Li Ki,* bk. iii, p. 241.

[3] *Confucian Analects,* bk. i, ch. v, p. 4.

[4] *Ibid.*

[5] *The Doctrine of the Mean,* ch. xx, sec. xiv.

[6] *Yi King,* appendix i, sec. ii, LX: 4.

follows: (i) Sufficient provisions for the decent maintenance of the aged, the widowed, the orphaned, and other unfortunates should first be made;[1] (ii) the system of universal education should be enforced;[2] (iii) the public appreciation of music and fine arts should be cultivated;[3] (iv) the use of parks and other places for popular amusement and recreation should be granted to the public;[4] (v) the livelihood of the people should be so regulated that they might have leisure to cultivate propriety and righteousness;[5] (vi) the administration of justice should be coordinated with public education to the end that a legal utopia might be achieved in which the convicts would all become good citizens and no further violation of law would occur and no more punishment be imposed;[6] and (vii) a sufficient force of disciplined soldiers should be kept for the maintenance of domestic security and international peace.[7] All these may serve to illustrate the statement made by Confucius that a good government should be not only economical, but also humanitarian; that it should be not only efficient in its administration, but also honest in its purpose, keeping the promises made to the people, and disturbing as little as possible the economic life of society.[8]

The Relation between Revenue and Expenditure. — According to the Royal Regulations and the Constitution of

---

[1] *Li Ki*, bk. vii, secs. i and ii; also *The Works of Mencius*, bk. i, pt. ii, ch. v and bk. vii, pt. i, ch. xxii.

[2] *Confucian Analects*, bk. xv, ch. 38. *The Works of Mencius*, bk. i, pt. i, ch. iii, sec. x.

[3] *Li Ki*, bk. xvii, sec. iii, vol. xxiii.

[4] *The Works of Mencius*, bk. i, pt. ii, ch. ii, secs. i and ii.

[5] *Ibid.*, bk. i, pt. i, ch. vii, secs. xx to xxiv.

[6] *Chinese Classics*, vol. iii, pt. i, bk. i, ch. iii.

[7] *Confucian Analects*, bk. xii, ch. vii.

[8] *Ibid.*, bk. i, ch. v, p. 4.

the Chou dynasty, two of the most important fiscal documents approved by Confucius, the principles which should govern the relation between public revenue and public expenditure were three in number: (1) the principle of budget regulations, (2) the principle of determining the relation between public revenue and social income, and (3) the principle governing the various processes of fiscal administration. The Royal Regulations provided that the prime minister of the central government should determine at the close of each year the national expenditures for the coming year. When all the harvests had been gathered in, he announced the budgets for the various states, allotting these in accordance with the size of the state and the average grain production and the average expenditures of the whole empire over a period of thirty years.[1] The most important principle of the budget thus laid down was that the amount of the expenditure of a government should be regulated by the amount of its probable income.

The Royal Regulations emphasized the necessity of having a definite proportion of social income for use in an emergency. If in a state there was not accumulated a grain surplus sufficient for the maintenance of the population for nine years, the condition of that state was called one of insufficiency; if there was not enough for six years, the condition was considered one of emergency; if there was not enough for three years, it was held that the life of the state could no longer continue. The husbandry of three years was considered to give an overplus of food sufficient for one year; that of nine years, an overplus for three years. If in the course of each thirty-year period provisions were made for nine unproductive years, the people would have sufficient food for subsistence even though there might be

---

[1] *Cf. Li Ki*, bk. iii, p. 221.

bad years, drought and inundation.[1] Confucius taught, therefore, that the fiscal strength of a state lay in the economic strength of its people and that the best proof of the latter was the surplus stores which they were able to accumulate over a period of years. His insistence on the maintenance of a thirty-years' food supply was due to the fact that at the stage of economic development which China had then reached the people engaged chiefly in agriculture and had not learned how to prevent the evil effects of such destructive forces as flood or drought, and they must needs therefore have ample reserve.

As a necessary corollary to the regulation of revenue and expenditure, the Confucians dwelt much on the importance of the organization of fiscal administration and the accuracy and publicity of accounts. Accordingly the stipulations of the Constitution of the Chou dynasty read:

The prime minister, in the capacity of minister of finance, regulated all taxation,[2] all tribute [3] and all expenditure [4] as prescribed by law; his under-secretary assisted him in the execution of this work and in the auditing of the accounts submitted by the various government departments; under them the minister of accounts took charge of the examination of the minutes and receipts for the supervision and compilation of the daily, monthly and yearly accounts. The chief of the Bureau of Revenue had the custody of the imperial revenue and estimated the revenue of the next year, while the Bureau of Disbursements had charge of the imperial outlays.[5]

[1] *Cf. Li Ki*, bk. iii, p. 222.

[2] Sun I-jang, *Critical Interpretations on the Constitution of the Chou Dynasty*, ch. iii, folios 1-4.

[3] *Ibid.*, folios 6-8.

[4] *Ibid.*, folios 4-6.

[5] Constitution of the Chou dynasty, pt. i, pp. 8-9, 12-14 and pt. ii, pp. 10-14.

In the Royal Regulations we find this statement, "The minister of accounts shall prepare the complete accounts of the year to be submitted to the emperor, and these shall be received by the prime minister reverently." [1]   This was then considered as the final step in constitutional fiscal control, because, although the emperor was held responsible to the people at large according to the ancient Chinese political tradition,[2] the administrative responsibility rested first upon the heads of different departments, who were held accountable to the prime minister, while the latter was in turn responsible to the emperor.   This plan of administrative organization indicates that the development of constitutional monarchy had made a forward stride during the early part of the Chou dynasty, that the responsibility of the prime minister was well defined, and that the great Confucians in formulating their policies elaborated the fundamental principles of constitutional finance.

FISCAL CONTROVERSIES BETWEEN CONFUCIANS AND JURISTS AND CONFUCIAN-JURISTS

The controversies between the later Confucians and Jurists and between the orthodox Confucians and the Jurist-Confucians or neo-Confucians are full of interest.   In the year 81 A. D. an important dispute over the problem of salt and iron monopolies occurred between the Jurists, who advocated the monopolistic policy, and the Confucians, who strongly took the opposition.[3]   A work entitled *A Debate on the Government Monopoly of Salt and Iron,* giving the various arguments on both sides of this controversy, was written by Huan K'uan during the reign of Emperor Hsüan of the Former Han dynasty (73-49 B. C); and this is considered a valuable contribution to Chinese fiscal literature.

[1] *Li Ki,* bk. iii, p. 239.

[2] *The Works of Mencius,* bk. v, pt. i, chs. v and vi.

[3] *Infra,* pp. 76-78.

In 794 A. D., Lu Chih, one of the greatest statesmen of the T'ang dynasty, elaborated a theory of taxation, basing it entirely upon orthodox Confucian fiscal doctrines, and directing his attacks against the liberal measures introduced by a contemporary financier, Yang Yeh, for the reform of land taxation.[1] Yang Yeh, though technically a Confucian, was in reality a practical statesman more of the Jurist type, and this controversy may therefore be properly considered one between the orthodox Confucians and the Jurist-Confucians.

The warfare between the conservative Confucians and the neo-Confucians over fiscal problems reached its climax in the middle of the Northern Sung dynasty. The noted leader of the latter party was Wang An-shih (1021-1086 A. D.), who attempted a number of fiscal reforms, the most outstanding of which was the abolition of the personal service tax, one of the most onerous types of taxation.[2] His reform measures, however, were chiefly based upon the Constitution of the Chou dynasty, notwithstanding that his interpretation was a liberal one.

After this neo-Confucian school lost its influence, the orthodox Confucians held greater sway than ever before, and traditionalism became the rule of educated society, with the inevitable decline of critical thinking in general, and of scientific study of public finance in particular. Although there was established by Yeh Shih (1150-1223 A. D.) a school called Yungchia,[3] the avowed object of which was the systematic study of political and economic problems, its influence soon disappeared after the death of its founder, and thereafter the orthodox Confucians· contented themselves with being expounders of traditional fiscal doctrines rather than original thinkers.

[1] *Infra,* pp. 88-91.

[2] *Infra,* p. 101.

[3] The name of a district of the province of Chekiang, the birthplace of Yeh Shih.

THE CAUSES OF THE STAGNATION OF FISCAL STUDY
EXAMINED

The main causes of the stagnation of fiscal study from the time of Emperor Wu of the Former Han dynasty are nine in number. The first of these was the influence of 100 per cent Confucianism and the consequent extreme conservatism which prevailed. Emperor Han Wu adopted the monopolistic fiscal measures of the Jurists and, at the same time, elevated Confucianism to the position of the national orthodox religion in order that the two leading schools of his time might render whatever service each of them could best contribute. But the result was that the fiscal policy of the school of Jurists established itself in the Chinese fiscal system and was followed from that time on with few modifications or exceptions, the Confucians either tacitly admitting the advisability of the monopolistic policy of the opponent school or contenting themselves with a display of disappointment at the impossibility of restoring the ancient ideal or utopian system of state-ownership of land together with its equitable distribution. For the most part, the fiscal policy of raising the greatest revenue with the least trouble by practising monopolistic measures was recognized as a proper course for the state to take, and this monopolistic policy coupled with the tithe on the produce of land became a part of the traditional fiscal program of the statesmen who were Jurists or Confucian-Jurists in reality, but generally orthodox Confucians in name. On the side of state expenditure, however, the schools of Lao Tzŭ and Confucius still exercised a great influence in limiting the expansion of the sphere of governmental functions. The schools of Mo Ti and the Agriculturalists no longed played an important part in the determination of fiscal policies after the Confucianization of the whole empire by Han Wu.

Second, as a result of the policy of minimum interference

as advocated by the school of Lao Tzŭ, the fiscal problem could not be made a focus of popular discussion, inasmuch as the development of fiscal science depends largely on popular interest in such problems as taxation, public debts, or tariff revision, which are of vital importance to society at large.

Third, most of the Chinese scholars, whose attitude was not very different from that of the ancient philosophers of Greece and Rome, inclined to underestimate the importance of economic considerations in order to emphasize the concerns of spiritual and moral life. This attitude of anti-materialism played an important role in diverting the attention of the scholars from the field of economic or fiscal studies.

Fourth, as pointed out at the very beginning of this essay, the Chinese historians paid much attention to the scientific treatment, of fiscal development, the most noteworthy being Sŭ-ma Ch'ien, Pan Ku, Tu Yu, Ssŭ-ma Kuang, and Ma Tuan-lin; but not one of them confined himself to the treatment of fiscal subjects. Although Tu Yu's *History of Political Institutes,* and Ma Tuan-lin's *General Researches on Political Institutions and Literary Authorities* afford us a mass of material for study along the lines of public revenues, public expenditures and monetary systems, the subject of public finance was considered merely as a branch of political history, and this conception of its dependence upon history made the Chinese scholars more inclined to approach their fiscal investigations from the historical point of view than from the angle of ideological research.[1] For this

---

[1] For example, Ku Yen-wu (1612-1681 A. D.), Huang Tsung-hsi (1609-1695), and Wang Fu-chih (1627-1679) were the three great Confucians of the seventeenth century. Ku Yen-wu and Wang Fu-chih made invaluable contributions to the study of Chinese political and economic history, while Huang Tsung-hsi expounded the social contract theory of the origin of state in his book entitled "An Appeal for a Better World." They, however, threw no new light on Chinese fiscal philosophy.

reason, their discussions centered around the possibilities of restoring the ancient systems instead of developing something new, and their research work was concerned chiefly with fiscal history instead of with fiscal theory.

Fifth, China has been an agricultural nation for a long time; and, as a rule, an agricultural society is most favorable to the fixation of the law of taxation, and most unfavorable to an increase of the land tax. This is shown by the fact that the one-tenth tax on the produce of the land has been accepted, in principle at least, from the time of Yü the Great up to the present—a period of more than forty centuries. The conservatism on the part of the general public explains, at least in part, why a progressive and thorough fiscal reform is usually not welcomed by the mass of the property-holding class and why the attempts at such reforms, as history shows, have to a large extent ended in failure.

Sixth, the non-development of commercial and manufacturing enterprises has made the imposition of taxes other than those on salt, iron, and similar necessities of life almost impossible; for no worthy scholar would wish to burden with further taxation the poorer classes, who are already over-taxed.

Seventh, as political scientists tell us, the monopolistic policy as a fiscal measure has the same result as indirect taxation, and weakens the sense of political responsibility on the part of the people, and hence their interest in fiscal discussions.

Eighth, the lack of publicity of government accounts has also been one of the technical hindrances to the development of a fiscal science.

Ninth, and most important, was the lack of a constitutional government [1] after the Chou dynasty. Because of

[1] This term is used in its broad sense.

this, the government revenue and the royal revenue were not separated, with some exceptions when an economist-ruler or a great financier was in power. Moreover, the people at large had no part in determining national fiscal policies. Such matters were in the hands of a group of scholars usually chosen through competitive examinations and prepared for government service. It is quite natural then that this people, without representation in the national government and without voice in its fiscal affairs should cling to the conviction that the least government is the best government and the least taxation is the best taxation. The Chinese have a far greater trust in their village and guild governments than in any other administrative organization, because these two forms of government are conducted far more directly by themselves.

FISCAL RESEARCH FROM A NEW VIEWPOINT

Several factors are combining to eliminate the various deterrents to the development of fiscal study: (1) The critical spirit of the Chinese intellectual class has experienced a rebirth through the influence of Western science on the original Chinese culture. (2) The people are developing an interest in the study of fiscal problems as a result of their fuller participation in their district, provincial and national governments since the establishment of the Republic. (3) The gradual and moderate expansion of government functions becomes a matter of necessity as the modernized cities spring up one after the other. (4) The close relation between public finance and socio-economic welfare has been recognized. (5) The necessity for the reform of the land tax system is accepted as exceedingly urgent. (6) The abolition of taxes on salt and other necessities is considered merely a question of time by the advocates of fiscal justice.

(7) The imposition of direct taxation in the form of an income tax or an inheritance tax as a substitute for the harmful forms of *likin* or internal transit duties is being recommended by the leading economists and statesmen of the country.   (8) The effective control of the public purse is coming to the fore as the chief problem of real democratic government.   (9) The publicity of accounts is urgently demanded by commercial organizations and other representative bodies of the people; and through this publicity the responsibility of the administrative officers to their constituents will be secured, the public at large or the tax-payers in particular will become better informed, and, above all, statistical data for scientific fiscal research will become more abundant in quantity, more reliable in quality, and more easily accessible for an increasingly larger number of scholars who are especially concerned with the study of practical fiscal problems.   (10) The prompt abolition of unjustifiable treaty restrictions on China's taxing powers and the complete restoration of tariff autonomy have come very recently to be fully recognized as necessary steps for the increase of national revenue and the protection of home industries.

China is ready for a modern democratic system of finance, without which no democratic government is possible.   It is our opinion that the fiscal principles laid down by the ancient Chinese philosophers may be applied with excellent advantage in the formulation of a scientific and practical system, and that the fiscal experiments which the country has made throughout her history will serve to show the course to be followed and the pitfalls to be avoided.   We shall therefore pass on to a brief historical survey of the development of the Chinese fiscal system.

PART TWO

A Brief Survey of the Fiscal Development of China, or A Fiscal Interpretation of China's Political Evolution

The whole course of Chinese fiscal history may be divided into three main periods coinciding with the three stages of political development through which the country has passed: (a) the Feudal Period (2698-221 B. C.), (b) the Imperial Period (221 B. C.–1912 A. D.), and (c) the Republican Period (1912 A. D.....).

THE FEUDAL PERIOD (2698-221 B. C.)

Development of the Public Land System. — During the greater part of the period preceding the establishment of the Ch'in dynasty in the year 221 B. C., a feudal régime was in force throughout China; the land was in the hands of the state, and the *tsing tien* or public land system prevailed. It has been generally held by the Chinese historians that the *tsing tien* system was based on the feudal system, and that both of these owed their origin to Emperor Huang (about 2698 B. C.), the founder of the Chinese Empire. This ruler mapped out the whole country into provinces, and set up 10,000 states, each 100 *li*[1] square. He called the area of each square *li* one *tsing*. Within the limits of each *tsing*, four roads were built; one well (also called a *tsing* in Chinese) was dug in the center, and around that well eight

[1] A *li* is about four-tenths of an English statute mile.

49

buildings were provided for the eight families who were assigned to live in the area and till the land allotted to them.[1] Thus the people were entitled not only to cultivate the public land (*tien*), deriving therefrom their supplies of food and clothing, but also to use public buildings for their dwellings and public wells (*tsing*) for their water-supply. This is one of the reasons why the system was termed *tsing tien*. Another reason is that the public land system is best illustrated by the Chinese character 井 (*tsing,* meaning a well), because when the character is enclosed in a square, like this,

nine inner squares are formed, the square in the center representing the public field, and the eight surrounding it, private fields. This interpretation was, however, of later origin, as the distinction between the public and the private field was not made until the Yin dynasty (1766-1122 B. C.). The conditions on which the land was allotted during the reign of Emperor Huang are not definitely known. The most acceptable explanation is that a tribute system existed similar in great measure to that employed during the subsequent Hsia dynasty (2205-1766 B. C.).

Beginning with the Hsia dynasty, the *tsing tien* system passed through three phases of development: that of the tribute system, during the Hsia Dynasty (2205-1766 B. C.), that of the aid system, during the Yin Dynasty (1766-1122 B. C.), and that of the share system, during the Chou Dynasty (1122-221 B. C.). According to Mencius, a land tax of one-tenth of the produce of the land was exacted throughout the three dynasties.

The Hsia Dynasty allotted fifty *mou,* or Chinese acres, to a

---

[1] *Chinese Classics,* vol. iii, pt. i, p. 93.

man, he said, and he paid the produce of five *mou* in the form
of tribute; the Yin Dynasty allotted him seventy *mou*, and he
paid the yield of seven *mou* under the name of aid; the Chow
Dynasty allotted him one hundred *mou*, and he paid the yield
of ten *mou* as his share toward the government revenue.
Thus, the tax system of these dynasties was as a matter of
fact merely a tithe.[1]

This gives in brief the distinguishing characteristic of
each of the three systems. Let us now consider each system
somewhat in detail.

*The Tribute System of the Hsia Dynasty (2205-1766
B. C.).*—As provided by the fiscal system of Yü the Great,
the founder of the Hsia dynasty, there were two main
sources of imperial revenue during that dynasty, namely,
taxes and tribute. The former was the name given to those
land taxes which were paid by the people directly to either
the imperial or the feudal government, while the latter denoted the revenue received by the central government, not
directly from the people themselves in the form of taxation,
but indirectly through the feudal princes in the form of
tribute.

In view of the fact that the central feature of this system,
which is known as the " tribute system of Yü," was the
regulation of the tax on land, Professor James Legge, the
well-known English authority on Chinese classical works,
suggested that it might be better styled the " taxation system of Yü." [2] But, strictly speaking, the system covered
both tribute and taxation, and inasmuch as neither of these
should be overlooked, the most appropriate name for it
would be the " tribute and taxation system of Yü the
Great ". The term " tribute system of Yü " is, however, a

[1] *Chinese Classics*, vol. ii, pp. 240-241.
[2] *Ibid.*, vol. iii, pt. i, p. 93.

satisfactory designation. In the first place, it has the essential qualities of brevity and conciseness. In the second place, history shows that eight out of the nine provinces then constituting the major political divisions of the Middle Kingdom, were taxed by the central government through the medium of tribute, and that only in the province of Ki, i. e., the domain under the direct control of the imperial government, was the land tax levied and collected by the central government itself. In other words, only one-ninth of the area of the whole Empire was subject to direct taxation by the central government, whereas in eight-ninths of that area taxes were levied indirectly under the name of feudal tribute.

Since the system of Yü was the most ancient form of Chinese public finance, some of its special features are worth noting. It provided first for the classification of land into nine grades according to its quality. After bringing under control an unprecedented inundation of the Yellow River, Yü the Great made a nation-wide survey to determine the types of land existing throughout the Empire. On the basis of his findings, land was divided into three classes, each with a threefold subdivision, making in all nine classes. This method of classification has constituted, ever since, the fundamental principle of land taxation in China, and it is only in very recent times that a change of basis for the levying of the land tax has been suggested.[1]

Under the system of Yü, fifty *mou* of the first class land were allotted to each husbandman, a term denoting the head of a family consisting of five members. The husbandman was required to pay to the state as a tax the produce of five of the fifty *mou*. The amount of his yearly tax was fixed on a basis of the average yield of the land over a period of years.[2] The revenue thus obtained was divided between the

[1] *Infra*, p. 154, footnote. See also *infra*, p. 57.
[2] *Chinese Classics*, vol. ii, pp. 240-241.

imperial and the feudal governments. In the imperial domain, the land tax was paid in products of the soil and
directly to the central government; in the feudal states, it
was paid not to the central government, but to the feudal
princes, who retained a fixed proportion of this revenue to
defray the expenses of their governments and took the rest
in order to buy the most distinctive and highly prized products of their states, which they sent to the central government as their tribute to the emperor. The reasons for this
arrangement were two: first, the economic life of that time
was still in a stage of barter, so that the feudal princes had
to share their revenues with the central authority by supply-
ing merchandise for the use of the latter; second, the precious articles of tribute were, as a rule, less bulky and less
heavy than the ordinary agricultural products of the various
states, and therefore the cost of transportation could be
greatly lessened by sending the choicer articles. This system then may be properly styled one of governmental bartering, or barter finance, and was a legitimate result of the
primitive barter economy. It is also worthy of notice that
this system marked the first recorded step in the division of
revenue between the central and the local governme: t in
China.[1]

For the purpose of distinction, Dr. Chen Huan-chang has
called the tribute a tax paid in value instead of in kind.[2]
Our suggestion would be to entitle the land tax proper of
that time the " direct land tax," and the tribute, the " indirect land tax," because the source of these two types of
imperial revenue was one, namely, the produce of the land.

[1] For the proportion of their revenue which the feudal states were
authorized to retain, see Chen Huan-chang, *op. cit.*, p. 640.

[2] Chen Huan-chang, *op. cit.*, p. 640.

For the regulation of feudal tribute, Yü the Great laid down the general principle that the feudal states be required to furnish as tribute only such articles as were produced within their boundaries, and it was only in exceptional cases that products of neighboring domains which could be purchased without much difficulty might be included in the list of commodities assigned to various states.[1] The object of this provision was to prevent the imperial government from exacting those articles of tribute which were difficult to obtain.

With regard to the jurisdiction of the tribute system, a distinction was made between regular or compulsory tribute and irregular or voluntary tribute. The former denoted such tribute as was required of, and regularly paid by, the feudal states scattered throughout the Middle Kingdom, while the latter was that which was occasionally and voluntarily paid by the barbarian tribes then living outside of its boundaries. This shows that compulsory tribute was limited to the domain which had attained the status of feudal states.

Shortly before the establishment of the Hsia dynasty a study was made of the relationship existing between the quality of land in the several provinces and the amount of revenue derived from the land tax in those provinces. The data presented in the following table show the disparity which was found to obtain between the former and the latter.[2]

[1] *Chinese Classics*, vol. iii, pt. iii, pp. 92-151.
[2] *Ibid.,* vol. iii, pt. iii, pp. 92-151.

RATING OF NINE PROVINCES OF THE MIDDLE KINGDOM AS TO QUALITY OF
LAND AND REVENUE DERIVED FROM LAND TAXES

Provinces	Rating as to Quality of Land	Rating as to Annual Revenue derived from Land Taxes
Yung Chow	A1 (1st grade)	B3 (6th grade)
Sü Chow	A2 (2nd grade)	B2 (5th grade)
Ts'ing Chow	A3 (3rd grade)	B1 (4th grade)
Yü Chow	B1 (4th grade)	A2 (2nd grade) or in some years A1 (1st grade)
Ki Chow	B2 (5th grade)	A1 (1st grade) or in some years A2 (2nd grade)
Yên Chow	B3 (6th grade)	C3 (9th grade)
Liang Chow	C1 (7th grade)	C2 (8th grade) or in some years C3 (9th grade), C1 (7th grade), or B3 (6th grade)
King Chow	C2 (8th grade)	A3 (3rd grade)
Yang Chow	C3 (9th grade)	C1 (7th grade) or in some years C2 (8th grade)

It will be seen that among the nine provinces, there were
five in which the quality of land was rated higher than the
amount of revenue derived from the tithe on the produce
of land, namely, Yung Chow, Shü Chow, Ts'ing Chow, Yên
Chow, and Liang Chow; whereas in four the quality of the
land was rated lower than the annual revenue derived from
the produce, namely, Yü Chow, Ki Chow, King Chow, and
Yang Chow.

In the provinces Yung Chow and King Chow the disparity between the quality of land and the annual amount
of land-tax revenue was as great as five grades. In the
former province the land was of the first grade, but its
revenue-yielding capacity was of the sixth grade. In the

latter province, on the contrary, the land was of the eighth grade, whereas its revenue-yielding capacity was of the third grade. Yung Chow presented the phenomenon of land of high grade producing a small proportion of the total revenue of the country, and Ki Chow that of a low grade of land producing a large proportion of the total revenue. In the province of Ki Chow there was a disparity of four grades between the quality of land and the revenue derived from it; in other words, fifth-grade land had a revenue-yielding capacity of first or, in some years, second grade. In the case of Sü Chow and Yên Chow the rating in quality of land exceeded by three grades the rating in revenue-yielding capacity. The least disparity between quality of land and revenue-yielding capacity was found in the provinces of Ts'ing Chow and Liang Chow, where third-grade land yielded revenue of the fourth grade and the seventh-grade land yielded revenue of the eighth grade. In no instance did a province receive the same grade in quality of land and revenue-yielding capacity.

Investigations showed that two main factors determined the productiveness of the land, the one dynamic, i. e., the supply of labor, the other static, i. e., the supply of land. In the case of the province of Yung Chow, it was found that land of high quality yielded a low revenue because of the sparsity of the population, while in the province of King Chow, the land yielded a high revenue despite its inferior quality because it was well populated. The government sought to deal with these conditions by adjusting the supply of land to the supply of labor through distributing groups of the residents from the overpopulated districts throughout the districts which were underpopulated, thus making it possible for every able-bodied citizen to be employed in the cultivation of land and for every piece of farm land to become productive to the utmost degree.

Especial attention was still paid to the equal distribution of land and population during the succeeding dynasties, Yin and Chou, when the *tsing tien* system remained in force. Moreover, it is evident that the importance of land and population in their relation to public finance was more or less continually recognized by the Chinese government from the Chou dynasty down to the establishment of the Republic, for the department of finance was often designated as the " Ministry of Land " or " Board of Population " instead of " Board of Estimates and Appropriations," although the latter name was also sometimes employed.[1]

The tribute system had long been abolished, but its two guiding principles, viz., the division of the land into nine classes according to its quality and the exaction of one-tenth of the produce of the land as a tax, constituted the backbone of the tax system approved by Confucius and his school and still hold good today. So, in a certain sense, the tribute system of Yü may be well called the permanent Chinese fiscal constitution. The system, however, was severely criticized by Lung Tzŭ,[2] an ancient philosopher holding nearly the same views as the school of Agriculturalists which, as has been pointed out,[3] supported land nationalization and cooperative farming. The comments made by him and quoted by Mencius read as follows:

. . . For regulating the administration of public land, there is no system which is worse than that of tribute. Under this system, the regular amount of taxation is fixed on a basis of the average yield of the land over a period of several years. In

[1] *General Research,* ch. 52; *Continuation of General Research,* chs. 51-52; *Political Institutes of the Ts'ing Dynasty,* ch. 24.

[2] Sometimes called Lung Shu. Quoted in *Lieh Tzŭ,* chapter on Confucius. See also Shao Chin, *An Interpretation of the Philosophy of Mencius,* vol. x, p. 42.

[3] See *supra,* p. 23.

good years, when the grains are plenty, much may be taken without inconvenience to the landholder; but the actual levy is not increased in due proportion to the harvest. In bad years, when the produce may not be sufficient to repay the expense of fertilizing the fields, and the fixed amount of taxation must still be paid in full, the system becomes oppressive.[1]

Many Chinese scholars, including Dr. Chen Huan-chang, contend that what Lung Tzŭ meant by the system of tribute was not the system of the Hsia dynasty, but the practice of the Warring States (403-221 B. C.). It is plain, however, that Mencius quoted the statement of Lung Tzŭ in order to show the comparative superiority of the aid and the share systems over the system of tribute, and he would not have cited the passage had it had no reference to the system of the Hsia dynasty.

Although the tribute system failed to comply with the principle of justice in that it taxed property in proportion to area instead of to net revenue, it nevertheless possessed the merit of simplicity and could be easily administered. Furthermore, its defects were not grave ones, when the method of tilling the soil was primitive and the expenses of cultivation were fairly uniform. But it could not be readily adjusted to the changing net revenue of property; and there was difficulty, too, in revising the classifications of the holdings which usually changed with improvement in the methods of cultivation. Accordingly this system finally gave way to the aid system when the Yin dynasty began to play its rôle.

The Aid System of the Yin Dynasty (1766-1122 B. C.).
—According to Chu Hsi (1130-1200 A. D.), the greatest Confucian scholar of the Sung dynasty, the aid system of

---

[1] *Chinese Classics*, vol. ii, pp. 241-242.

[2] Chen Huan-chang, *op. cit.*, p. 623, foot-note.

the Yin dynasty required that all land susceptible of cultivation be divided into lots of 630 *mou* each, and that each of these in turn be subdivided into nine squares of seventy *mou* each, and allotted to eight families on condition that they cultivate the square in the center of the lot in common and give its produce to the government as a tax.[1] The central lot was known as the public field and the eight surrounding lots as private fields. As the public field was cultivated by the cooperative labor of those who held the other eight lots, the rate of land taxation was, as a matter of fact, raised under this system from one-tenth to one-ninth.

The aid system was a remedy for the defects of the tribute system of the Hsia dynasty. But where the tribute system, with its tax of a fixed percentage on the gross produce of each husbandman's holdings, was profitable to the government, although not necessarily to the people, the aid system was of advantage to the people, but not necessarily to the state. It was advantageous to the people because they had to contribute their labor only for the cultivation of the public field and were not responsible for the losses of a bad year. It might be disadvantageous to the state inasmuch as the people might be driven by selfish motives to devote most of their capital and labor to the cultivation of their private fields, and thus leave the public field poorly tended. It is true, however, that if the government is good, the people are usually faithful to it, and sometimes, possibly, care more for the public interests than for their own. An ode in the *Canon of Poetry* says: " May it rain first on our public fields, and then come to our private holdings." [2] Such sentiments are, of course, exceptional; but it is fairly certain that the aid, or as we may better call it the cooperative, system strengthened the relationship between the government and

[1] *Chinese Classics,* vol. ii, pp. 240-241.

[2] *Ibid.,* vol. iv, pt. ii, p. 381.

the people and developed a sense of mutual responsibility. In Ku Liang's *Commentary on Spring and Autumn,* we find this statement: " When the crop of the private fields is not good, the officials should be blamed; when that of the public fields is not good, the people are at fault." [1]

The Share System of the Chou Dynasty (1122-221 B. C.). —According to the interpretation of Chu Hsi, the Chou dynasty adopted a tax program which combined the two preceding systems, employing the tribute system for the urban districts and the aid system for the rural areas.[2] It has been pointed out, however, by Yü Yueh, the late director of the Institute for Chinese Classical Research, that under the new system the central public field ceased to exist on account of the fact that during that period each eight families were allotted nine hundred *mou* for cultivation, and the government was privileged to claim at its own discretion the produce of any hundred *mou* out of every nine hundred.[3] Thus the system which was known as the share, or assessment, system was really a scheme devised to guard against the possibility of the cultivators' devoting more attention to their private holdings than to the public field.

Other Forms of Revenue.—During the Chou dynasty, the male citizens were required to pay a personal service tax in addition to that of grain, and the female citizens, a tax of hempen-cloth. Regarding the payment of these taxes, Mencius made the following recommendations:

There are three exactions necessary for the support of the state: the exaction of grain, of hempen-cloth, and of personal

[1] Annotation on the Record of Events in the fifteenth year of Duke Hsüan.

[2] *Cf. Chinese Classics,* vol. ii, pp. 240-241.

[3] Yü Yueh, *Critical Comments on Ancient Chinese Classics,* vol. 32, pp. 27-28.

service. The ruler should require only one of these at a time, deferring the other two. If he demands two of them at once, the people will suffer; if he requires all three at once, families will be broken up, and fathers and sons will be separated.[1]

This was in reality a canon of taxation emphasizing that the ability of the people to pay and their convenience in doing so should be given especial attention.

It was usually maintained by the Confucian school that the exactions of grain should be paid after the harvest and that of the hempen-cloth in summer, while the personal services of the men were to be given for public work during the leisure of winter. The number of days which a man was asked to work for the government varied according to the condition of the crops of each year. The rules given in the fourth chapter of the Constitution of the Chou Dynasty [2] on this point were as follows: " In a good year, the period required for public work is three days; in an ordinary year, two days; and in a bad year, one day. If there is famine or epidemic, there will be no requirement of personal service." The reasons for the latter provision were two: first, it was felt that the people should be released from any service other than that needed for their own preservation during the bad years or years of famine; and, second, no public work would be undertaken when the people were in straitened circumstances except that purposely projected for the relief of these circumstances.

It is generally believed that the personal service tax and the tax on hempen-cloth were features of the taxation system of the Yin dynasty which the Chou dynasty borrowed and incorporated in its own system. With the development of economic life a number of new taxes came into

---

[1] *Chinese Classics*, vol. ii, bk. vii, pt. ii, ch. 27.

[2] Biot, *Tcheou-li*, vol. i, bk. xiii, pp. 290-291. See also Chen Huan-chang, *op. cit.*, pp. 663-664.

existence. The Constitution of the Chou Dynasty classified
the occupations of the people of the time as follows: (1)
farming, (2) horticulture, (3) forestry, mining and fishery,
(4) poultry- and stock-raising, (5) handicrafts, (6) commerce and trade, (7) silk-making and cloth-weaving, (8)
homekeeping, (9) transportation and other kinds of general
labor.[1] Every citizen, whether male or female, was required
by the Constitution to engage in some one of these industries. For the regulation and inspection of the various occupations a number of new administrative offices were created.
Other lines of governmental administration such as judiciary
and military functions grew in volume. As a result, the
government expenses increased enormously, and the imposition of new taxes became a matter of necessity. Chief
among those exacted were customs, business taxes and taxes
on mining, forestry and fisheries. Revenue was also secured
from the sale of surplus government supplies.

The customs system of the Chou dynasty was derived
from that of the Yin dynasty, but it differed from the latter
in that it was a system of revenue, while the latter was
merely one of inspection designed to prevent the entrance
into the country of persons or goods that might be undesirable from the standpoint of public policy. According to the
Constitution of the Chou dynasty, commodities were taxed
at one, and only one, of the following places, namely, external customs-houses, internal customs-houses, and market
places. When a merchant imported a commodity into the
country, he was required to pay a certain amount of import
duty. On making this payment, he was given a receipt which
he was required to present to the officers in charge of the
internal customs-houses and market-places for examination.
When he exported a commodity, he paid an export duty to

[1] Biot, *op. cit.*, vol. i, bk. ii, pp. 26-27.

the controller of the market and received from the latter a receipt for this amount. When the commodity passed through internal and external customs-houses, it was required that the receipt be shown to the officers thereof.[1]

The business dues were of three main kinds: (1) taxes on business firms; (2) fees collected (a) from the sale of weights and measures, and (b) for the use of warehouses; and (3) fines imposed (a) upon persons who committed fraud or evaded responsibility in their credit transactions,[2] and (b) upon those who disobeyed the instructions of the controller or inspector of the market.[3]

Revenues from such industries as mining, forestry, fisheries, and the sale of surplus government supplies were collected by special officials. In addition to the taxes, fees and fines mentioned above, occupational tributes were exacted from those who had fixed professions, and fines were laid upon those who failed to do their work in accordance with government requirements. The latter were levied, not for the purpose of revenue, but rather to encourage industry and to enforce the laws of compulsory labor in regular and fixed occupations.

The occupational tributes, like the tribute of the feudal princes, were paid in kind. Only persons who were engaged in the business of transportation and general labor made payment in money. The people were also required on occasion to supply the government with war horses, chariots and oxen so that the military preparedness of the nation might be assured.

[1] Biot, *op. cit.*, vol. i, pp. 314, 329, 331-332. See also Chen Huan-chang, *op. cit.*, pp. 683-684.

[2] Credit transactions were made at this time by means of written tallies or credit bills of silk or cloth.

[3] Sun I-jang, *op. cit.*, ch. 27, folios 9-12.

Money and Banking Systems.—With the greater development of commerce and industry, the use of money for the payment of customs duties, business taxes and other forms of public exactions became not uncommon, and the demand for a better monetary and credit system naturally presented itself. According to Tü Yu [1] and Ma Tuan-lin,[2] two of the foremost Chinese historians, the use of money in China dates back to the reign of Tai-hao, in the twenty-ninth century B. C. These writers stated that the money of the dynasties of Hsia and Yin was of two main kinds: the one metallic, the other non-metallic. The metallic money was of three grades, gold, silver and copper, and was cast in the forms of the *tao*, or the knife-shaped money, the *pu*, or the belt-shaped money, and the *ch'ien*, or the round money. The non-metallic money consisted of pearls, jewels and cowry-shells.

In the early part of the Chou dynasty Chiang T'ai-kung, the founder of the state of Ch'i and a celebrated economist-statesman of the time, formulated the monetary laws for the coinage of the cash or copper money, which was round in shape with a square hole in the center to permit the stringing together of as many coins as the people chose. Usually a string contained such a round number as 1,000 pieces of cash. He also introduced a gold money unit called the *chin* or Chinese catty, which was a cubic *ts'un* or Chinese inch in size. This early monetary system was gradually broken down after the lapse of a few hundred years. But in the seventh century B. C. there arose another great economist-statesman, Kuan Tzŭ, a follower of Chiang T'ai-kung and the founder of the school of Jurists, with whose theories we have dealt in previous pages.[3] He revived the monetary

[1] *Research in Political Institutions*, ch. i.

[2] *General Research*, ch. ii.

[3] *Supra*, pp. 25-37.

system of his noted forerunner and made certain improvements such as fixing the forms of the various coins and the weight of the metals composing them.

During the greater part of the Chou dynasty there were, then, three grades of money, namely, the upper grade currency, consisting of both pearls and jewels, the intermediate grade, or gold, currency, and the lower grade, or copper, currency, consisting of belt-shaped, knife-shaped, or round coins. The popularity of copper coins was greatly increased through the reform of Kuan Tzŭ. The use of pearls, jewels and cowry-shells as money was prohibited by law in the year 216 B. C., when the feudalism of ancient China came to an end, and the first emperor of the Ch'in dynasty changed the three-grade system into a two-grade system, employing gold coins as standard money and copper coins as subsidiary money.[1]

The earliest form of banking in China was the system of loans and currency regulation prescribed in the Constitution of the Chou dynasty. As the entire economic system of that time was under government control, both the issue of currency and the making of loans were in the hands of the government. The Constitution provided that in years of famine or other emergencies no business taxes or customs duties were to be levied by the government, and that a greater amount of currency was to be issued in order to meet the needs of the people.[2]

The Ch'uan-fu or Bureau of Currency and Produce Exchange was authorized to give credit and make loans to the people and to buy up goods which at any given time proved unsalable. The loans were of two kinds, productive and

[1] *History of Han*, ch. xxiv, sec. ii, folio 1.

[2] Sun I-jang, *op. cit.*, vol. xxvii, folios 6-7.

consumptive. When viewed from the standpoint of interest, they may be classified as interest-bearing loans and non-interest-bearing loans. If the people wanted to borrow money from the Bureau for productive purposes, their cases were investigated with the aid of local officials, and the loans were made if it was deemed advisable. If they were in need of certain commodities for sacrificial or funeral rites, they were allowed to buy these commodities from the Bureau on credit without paying interest. The limit of time for the payment of sacrifice loans was ten days, while that for funeral loans was three months. Commentators differed as to the way in which the interest on the productive loans was met. The most generally accepted belief was that payment might be made in the product of the locality. For instance, if the locality was an agricultural district, the interest might be paid in farm products; and if it was a manufacturing town, payment might be made in manufactured goods. Another interpretation was that it might be paid by doing some personal service for the government. The Bureau furnished the general supplies of the government. At the end of each year the surplus commodities on hand were transmitted to the Bureau of Custody of the Finance Department.[1] This illustrates the barter character of the early banking system of ancient China.

Organization of Fiscal Administration. — An elaborate system of fiscal administration was also outlined in the Constitution of the Chou dynasty. This is believed to have been formulated by Chou Kung, the founder of the dukedom of Lu, and the forerunner of Confucius, and Chiang T'ai-kung, the Duke of Ch'i. Let us consider first the manner in which the fiscal administration was related to the central administration (or cabinet) and other departments of the government.

[1] Sun I-jang, *op. cit.,* ch. xxviii, folios 3-5.

The administration of the government of the Chou dynasty was delegated to a cabinet which included the heads of the following six departments: the minister of heaven, who was prime minister and minister of the interior and of finance; the minister of earth, or minister of land administration and of education; the spring minister, or minister of rites and religion; the summer minister, or minister of war; the autumn minister, or minister of justice; and the winter minister, or minister of public works and of labor.[1]

The fiscal administration was vested chiefly in twelve offices,[2] viz., the Grand Treasury, the Magazine for Jade (or other first-class precious articles), the Magazine of the Interior (for the custody of second-class precious articles), the Magazine of the Exterior (for the custody of third-class precious articles), the Bureau of Currency, the Magazine for the Utensils Used in Worship or Sacrifice, the Bureau of Revenue, the Bureau of Monetary Materials, the Magazine for Surplus Government Supplies, the Bureau of Disbursements, the Office of the Comptroller-General of Public Accounts, and the Office of the Superintendent of Census, Public Accounts and Official Documents.[3]

---

[1] Biot, *op. cit.*, vol. i, pp. 20, 192, 418 and vol. ii, pp. 162, 307, 456.

[2] Chinese historians have generally held that this fiscal administration was a system of nine magazines or treasuries. To the nine magazines, however, must be added the three important offices concerned respectively with the disbursements of the government, the auditing of the accounts, and the gathering, compiling and custody of public documents relating to land administration and other legal, economic and fiscal matters.

These detailed stipulations regarding the fiscal administration of the Chou dynasty have led some Chinese critics to believe that the Constitution of the Chou Dynasty was written partly by the Duke of Chou with the cooperation of contemporary statesmen; some interpolations were made in this document later by certain Confucians, Jurists or Confucian-Jurists.

[3] Biot, *op. cit.*, vol. i, p. 121, Grand Treasury; 124, Magazine for Jade; 127, Magazine of the Interior; 128, Magazine of the Exterior; 129, Comptroller-general of Public Accounts; 132, Superintendent of Census, Public

It is worthy of note that the fiscal administration was so centralized that nine out of the twelve fiscal offices were placed under the direct control and supervision of the prime minister, assisted by a vice-minister and an assistant minister, namely, the Grand Treasury, the magazines of jade, of the interior, of the exterior, and of surplus government supplies, the bureaus of disbursements and of revenue, the offices of the comptroller-general of public accounts and the superintendent of census, public accounts, and official documents. The Currency Bureau was under the direct control of the minister of land administration, because its functions as a farm-loan bank and an exchange of agricultural produce were closely related to the latter administration. The Magazine for the Utensils Used in Worship or Sacrifice was for obvious reason under the minister of rites and religion. The Bureau of Monetary Materials was placed under the supervision of the minister of justice, so that the mining law might be effectively enforced. From this brief survey of the organization of fiscal administration it will be seen that the division of governmental function was based upon the principles of technical efficiency and administrative responsibility. It is not difficult, therefore, to understand why the reign of the Chou dynasty lasted over eight hundred years and won the name of the Golden Age of ancient China.

Some Special Features of the Fiscal Constitution of the Chou Dynasty.—The most noteworthy fiscal regulations of the Chou dynasty have been dealt with in connection with the treatment of the fiscal philosophy of the Confucian school.[1] Some administrative principles still deserve our

Accounts and Official Documents; 134, Bureau of Revenue; 135, Bureau of Disbursements; 136, Magazine for the Surplus of Governmental Supplies; 480, Magazine for the Utensils used in Worship or Sacrifice; vol. ii, p. 361, Bureau of Monetary Materials and Other Mineral Products.

[1] *Supra*, pp. 37-42.

attention. Chief among these was the designation of special revenue for special expenditure. It was stated in the Constitution that the grand treasury should collect revenue from nine sources according to the law and should regulate the nine items of government expenditure in accordance with definite legal standards. For the collection of land taxes the imperial domain was divided into six districts, and the revenues from these districts formed six items of the regular revenue of the imperial government. These proceeds and those from three other sources, i. e., customs duties and market dues, taxes on forestry and fisheries, and the sale of surplus government supplies, were distributed as follows:

Items of Regular Revenue	*Items of Regular Expenditure*
Revenue from customs duties and market dues	Maintenance of royal household
Land tax from the 1st district	Diplomatic purposes
Land tax from the 2nd district	Military purposes
Land tax from the 3rd district	Salaries and pensions
Land tax from the 4th district	Public works
Land tax from the 5th district	Ceremonial presents
Land tax from the 6th district	Worship and sacrifice
Taxes on forestry and fisheries	Funerals and famine relief
Revenue from the sale of surplus government supplies	Complimentary donations of gifts

Thus a definite item of revenue was allotted for a definite expenditure so that the regular revenue of that item might approximately meet the regular expenditure for which it was provided.[1]

The second notable and interesting provision was the establishment of the order in accordance with which the sovereign was required to make his expenditures. This was as follows, first and foremost, for worship and sacrifice; second, for the entertainment of guests or other diplomatic

[1] Sun I-jang, *op. cit.*, ch. xi, folio 14; consult also Biot, *op. cit.*, vol. i, pp. 121-124.

purposes; third, for funerals or famine relief; fourth, for the food, clothing and other household expenditures of the emperor and his family; fifth, for public works; sixth, for ceremonial presents, chiefly for distinguished visitors to the imperial court; seventh, for salaries [1] and pensions for the various officials; eighth, for keeping the horses and oxen for military or other purposes; and ninth, for complimentary donations or gifts on certain occasions.[2]

The third important provision was that the feudal tributes and the occupational tributes should both be kept for meeting the special or irregular expenditures.[3] The fourth was that separate offices should be maintained for the collection, the custody and the disbursement of funds so that each might be held separately responsible for its specific work. Last but not least were the provisions that estimates of expenditures should be made under the direction of the prime minister;[4] that daily, monthly, and yearly accounts should be kept by the officers in charge of the collection, custody and disbursement of public revenues;[5] and that the comptroller-general should, by checking every ten days the accounts of the bureaus of revenue, custody and disbursements, keep

[1] According to the explanation of King Pang as quoted in Sun I-jang's *Critical Interpretations on the Constitution of the Chou Dynasty,* the salaries paid to the officials varied according to the harvest of the five staple crops. If in a year one of the crops failed, the official salaries would be reduced by one-fifth of the original amount; if two, three, or four crops failed, two-fifths, three-fifths, or four-fifths were to be deducted. In case all the crops failed, the government was permitted to pay only such minimum salaries as would barely suffice for the subsistence of its staff or personnel. See Sun I-jang, *op. cit.,* ch. iii, folio 5; consult also *The Works of Mo Tzŭ,* ch. v, folios 1-3.

[2] Sun I-jang, *op. cit.,* ch. iii, folios 4-5; see also Biot, *op. cit.,* vol. i, pp. 31-32.

[3] Sun I-jang, *op. cit.,* ch. xi, folio 15; Biot, *op. cit.,* pp. 123-124.

[4] Sun I-jang, *op. cit.,* ch. iii, folios 4-5.

[5] Sun I-jang, *op. cit.,* ch. vi, folio 8; Biot, *op. cit.,* vol. i, p. 63.

himself informed of the daily accomplishments of the various departments, and by checking their monthly and yearly accounts, keep in touch with their monthly and yearly accomplishments.[1] It was largely on the basis of these fiscal records that the annual and the triennial promotions of the various officers were made, and that government action as regards the continuation, the reform, or the abolition, of the institutions then in force was determined.[2]

FORCES BRINGING ABOUT THE TRANSITION FROM FEUDAL TO IMPERIAL FINANCE

Toward the end of the Chou dynasty, the *tsing tien* system, the cornerstone of the feudal structure, began to break down for three reasons, the first economic, the second fiscal, and the third political. The economic reason was that the population increased apace, whereas the supply of land was limited. In consequence, the land allotted to the poorer members of society was gradually absorbed by the rich and strong, and there arose a tyranny of the landlord, which brought about the discontent of the mass of the people.

The fiscal reason was that governmental expenses, especially those for military purposes, increased steadily as rivalry and competition among the feudal powers grew keener and keener. The revenue from the one-tenth tax on the produce of land proved entirely insufficient for the demands. The means adopted by the feudal princes of that period to raise money were either to increase the rate of the land tax, to encourage the maximum utilization of the land power by means of improved methods of production, or to let the people own as much land as they wished and develop it to

[1] Sun I-jang, *op. cit.*, ch. xii, folio 10; Biot, *op. cit.*, vol. i, p. 131.

[2] Sun I-jang, *op. cit.*, ch. xii, folios 10-13; Biot, *op. cit.*, vol. i, pp. 63, 131 and 133.

the fullest extent so that the revenue of the state might be increased in proportion to the increased production of the land. The first of these policies was adopted in the year 594 B. C. by Duke Hsuan of the state of Lu, who levied an extra tax of one-tenth on the produce of land in addition to the original tax of one-tenth or, in some cases, one-ninth, and thus in practice raised the rate of the land tax to more than two-tenths.[1] The second policy was successfully carried out by Li Kwei in the state of Wei; of this we have treated at sufficient length in connection with the fiscal policies of other Jurists.[2] The third policy was advocated by Shang Yang, the Jurist prime minister of the state of Ch'in. This statesman had the courage to adopt as his definite program the abolition of the deep-rooted system of *tsing tien*, thus ushering in a new era in Chinese fiscal history. In other words, he sought to introduce the principle of free competition into the socio-economic order in place of state control. In the year 350 B. C., an ordinance was issued by the Duke Hsiao of the state of Ch'in upon the recommendation of Shang Yang, providing that the buying and selling of land be henceforth allowed, and that no limitation be placed on the extent of individual holdings, thus making it possible for the people to utilize as much land as they themselves saw fit.[3]

The political cause responsible for the passing of the *tsing tien* system was the breaking down of feudalism. The *tsing tien* system depended for its survival upon the existence of a feudal régime with a number of hereditary and

---

[1] Tso's *Commentary*, vol. xxiv, folio 15; Ku-liang's *Commentary*, vol. xii, folio 22; Kung-yang's *Commentary*, vol. xvi, folios 18-22. See also Liang Chi-ch'ao, *Development of Political Thought in Ancient China*, pp. 93-94.

[2] See *supra*, pp. 34-35.

[3] *Historical Record*, ch. 68, folio 5; *History of Han*, ch. xxiv, sec. i, folio 2.

aristocratic land owners exercising semi-independent powers over their domains. Two forces inimical to the continuance of such a régime arose. The one was a strongly anti-aristocratic sentiment aroused by the attacks of certain great thinkers of the period on the abuses of the aristocratic form of government. The most representative of these thinkers was Chuang Tzŭ, who denounced mercilessly the aristocratic and feudal government then existing, saying that those who stole trifling articles such as hooks were put to death by the so-called laws, while those who stole a large kingdom were honored as kings or princes. "Are these offices of feudal princes not the factories of legalized robberies?" he asked.[1] The other was the growing recognition of the necessity for the unification of the whole empire under a centralized government in order that a stop might be put to the waste caused by the constant warfare between the different feudal states and that there might be peace throughout the country.[2]

Statesmen were divided as to the method of bringing about this centralization. One group, represented by Confucian statesmen, thought that it could best be achieved through democracy and pacifism. A second group, consisting chiefly of Jurists of the extreme type, placed its faith in autocracy and militarism. Finally the Jurist Shang Yang succeeded in putting into effect certain agrarian and militaristic policies which rendered the state of Ch'in sufficiently powerful to conquer the other feudal states;[3] and in 221

[1] *The Works of Chuang Tzŭ*, bk. iv, ch. x, folio 6.

[2] *Historical Record*, ch. vi, folio xii.

[3] The agrarian and militaristic measures successfully carried out by Shang Yang were centered in his immigration policy. As the state of Ch'in was sparsely populated and the three neighboring states were in a condition of over-population, he held that the advisable policy for the government of Ch'in was to induce the people of those states to emigrate into its territory by providing good farms and dwellings for them and

B. C. the whole Chinese empire was unified under the First
Emperor of the Ch'in dynasty. Thus the long-established
feudal régime was brought to an end and the period of imperial finance took its rise.

THE IMPERIAL PERIOD (221 B. C.–1912 A. D.)

Throughout the imperial period, the revenue from the
taxation on land still constituted the main source of government income. As the changes made in the system of land
taxation during this era should be given special consideration and preëminent position in the treatment of Chinese
fiscal development, we shall divide the period, for purposes
of discussion, into three stages: that from the Ch'in dynasty
to the middle of the T'ang dynasty (221 B. C.–779 A. D.),
that from the middle of the T'ang dynasty to the middle of
the Ming dynasty (780-1579 A. D), and that from the middle
of the Ming dynasty to the end of the T'sing dynasty (1580-
1912 A. D.).

*Fiscal Development from the Ch'in Dynasty to the Middle
of the T'ang Dynasty (216 B. C.–780 A. D.)*

At the outset of the period extending from the establishment of the Ch'in dynasty to the middle of the T'ang
dynasty, China, as we have seen, experienced the greatest
political and fiscal revolution of the middle part of her
national life. Politically, the country saw the termination
of the feudal system and the unification of the whole empire
under a highly centralized government. This experiment
of extreme centralization was, however, of short duration.
Fiscally, the *tsing tien* system was abolished, and a system

exempting them from military duties for three generations with the
definite object that the immigrants might thus be solely employed for
the cultivation of land and might help the native citizens in such a way
as to make it possible for the latter to devote themselves to military
expeditions.

of taxation based upon private, rather than public, ownership of property was instituted. In the course of the period
several important fiscal experiments were made, chief among
which were (1) the operation of government monopolies of
salt and iron, (2) government regulation of transportation
and price levels on a nation-wide scale, (3) the attempt at
land nationalization during the time of Wang Mang, (4) the
unification of the monetary system, (5) the centralization
of the auditing of public accounts during the Latter Han
dynasty, (6) the partially successful reintroduction of the
tsing tien system during the Tsin and the Northern Wei
dynasties, (7) the abolition of the salt tax during the Sui
dynasty, (8) the administration of the system of triple
taxation during the early part of the T'ang dynasty, and
(9) the reform of salt monopoly by Liu An in the middle
of the T'ang period.

In the year 216 B. C., about half a century after the abolition of the *tsing tien* system in the state of Ch'in, the First
Emperor of the Ch'in dynasty decreed that the people themselves should declare the amount of land which they then
possessed or cultivated, in order that a land tax might be
levied.[1] Since that time the people have been, with few exceptions, permitted to buy and sell land freely, and private
ownership of land has prevailed throughout the whole
country.

Powerful as the First Emperor of Ch'in was, his dynasty
lasted only fifteen years (221-206 B. C.). According to
Pan Ku, the author of the history of the Han dynasty, the
amount of land and poll taxes and revenue from salt and
iron monopolies collected during the Ch'in dynasty was
twenty times as great as that of the earlier part of the Chou
dynasty, and the exaction of personal service was thirty times

[1] *Historical Record*, ch. vi; also *General Research*, ch. i.

[2] *History of Han*, ch. xxiv, sec. i, folio 3.

as great.[2] This burden of excessive taxation brought about a popular uprising of the whole nation, and the militaristic and autocratic régime of the Ch'in dynasty was summarily overthrown.

The Government Monopoly of Salt and Iron.—After the overthrow of the Ch'in dynasty, the policy of strong centralization advocated by the school of Jurists lost ground, and the *laissez faire* policy of the school of Lao Tzŭ was adopted as a reactionary measure against the despotic rule of the Ch'in emperors. The land tax was made as low as one-thirtieth—one-third of the rate exacted during the early part of the Chou dynasty—and complete freedom was given to those engaged in enterprises of a monopolistic nature. As a result there arose a number of powerful capitalists or captains of industry who gained control of the production and distribution of the necessities of life. Monopolies of salt and iron became particularly oppressive.

During the reign of Emperor Wu of the Former Han dynasty (140-87 B. C.), the territory of the Empire was greatly enlarged by a number of military conquests, and the power of the dynasty reached its zenith. Increased domains and expenses necessitated increased revenue; and, to secure this, Sang Hung-yang, son of a shrewd and successful financier of the time and a scholar of the Jurist type, together with some iron and salt merchants of the time, proposed the establishment of a system of governmental monopolies of salt and iron after the model set by Kuan Tzŭ. Sang Hung-yang maintained that such natural monopolies as these should be wrested from individuals in order that the profit derived from them might be enjoyed by the government and the undue power of the capitalistic super-rulers might be checked. Emperor Wu adopted this recommendation, and in 115 B. C. he appointed Sang Hung-yang second secretary of the finance department with the power to put it into effect.

Fiscally speaking, the program was a success, but it brought no relief to the public. In fact, the people bitterly complained that they were obliged to pay higher prices for the salt and iron products manufactured under state management, and that the goods turned out were of bad quality and not even up to the standard set by the former private competitive business concerns.[1]

Government Regulation of Transportation and Price Levels.—Sang Hung-yang also introduced a system of government control of the transportation and distribution of the staple agricultural products of the country, with a view to securing and maintaining an equilibrium between the supply and demand of commodities. Although this system, like the system of salt and iron monopolies, owed its origin to Kuan Tzŭ, Sang Hung-yang showed his ability in carrying it out on a far larger scale than his forerunner had done in the state of Ch'i.

For the operation of this system a central government transportation office was established in the capital of the Empire and local transportation offices were opened in every district of every province or prefecture. The people of each district sent to their local office the merchandise due to the government as taxes, and the central office directed the shipment of this merchandise to the ports of the country where there was a demand for it. In even the most remote districts it was required that taxes be paid in the staple products of the locality rather than in money or in products obtained through exchange with the merchants, as had hitherto been done; for it was believed that only in this way could the prices of all products be kept at the normal level.

[1] *Historical Record*, ch. xxx, folios 8-18; *History of Han*, ch. xxiv, sec. ii, folios 2-4; see also Huan K'uan, *A Debate on the Government Monopoly of Salt and Iron, passim.*

All the general supplies needed by the government offices were to be purchased and distributed by the Bureau of Equal Transportation, a subordinate office of the Finance Department, for Sang Hung-yang held that the competitive and uncentralized purchases by local officials inflated prices and that the engagement of these officials in business for their own profit could not be checked unless a centralized efficient administrative supervision was maintained.

The prices of all commodities were to be controlled by the Bureau of Level Standard under the supervision of the Finance Department. When the price of a certain merchandise was high, it was to be sold; when the price was low, it was to be purchased. Thus the rich merchants could make no unreasonable profit, and prices would remain stable. Because by such procedure prices would be held down artificially, the system was called the " level standard."

This program, too, met with strong opposition from the people, who preferred to deal directly with the merchants. Finally through the influence of the Confucians, the policy of government regulation of transportation and price levels was abandoned. Sang Hung-yang's system of salt and iron monopolies remained in force, however, and, except for occasional periods of abolition or suspension, these monopolies constituted important elements of the fiscal fabric of the later dynasties.

Attempt at Land Nationalization during the Time of Wang Mang.—Wang Mang, who usurped the throne from the last emperor of the Former Han Dynasty, tried hard to resurrect all the laws and institutions which had long since been discarded as antiquated and impracticable. His guide in legislation was the Constitution of the Chou Dynasty, and his chief policy for economic and fiscal reorganization was the nationalization of land by confiscation. He declared:

Although the rate of the land tax during the Han dynasty was reduced to one-thirtieth of the produce, the cultivators of the soil are in a far worse condition than they were in the past when the rate of the tax was one-tenth, for now they have to pay the landlords as much as one-half of the produce as rent, while in the past they had to pay only one-tenth as tax. It is the rich land-owners that are benefited by the low tax rate, not the poor tenants. The only remedy is the redistribution of land by the government.[1]

Consequently he proclaimed in the year 9 A. D. that the land of the whole empire should be confiscated to the state and be called henceforth " imperial land ", that slaves should be emancipated and be known hereafter as " private dependents ", that neither land nor dependents should any longer be bought or sold, that families having fewer than eight members, but owning more land than one *tsing* or 900 Chinese acres, should distribute their land in excess of this amount among their relatives or townsmen and that those failing to obey this decree should be put to death. He called himself a " new emperor " or an " imperial reformer "; and in a certain sense his fight against the tyranny of the landed class and slave owners may be regarded as a struggle between state capitalism and humanitarianism on the one hand and private capitalism and slavery on the other. Unfortunately Wang Mang was more of a visionary scholar than a practical statesman. Admitting that the conditions described in his decree were the great evils of the time, the means by which he sought to rid the country of these evils at one stroke were ill-chosen. Moreover, the law which he formulated was not definitely worded; his administration was exceedingly inefficient and corrupt; and the fact of his usurpation discredited him among the people at large. The whole empire was soon set in disorder, and a revolutionary

[1] *History of Han*, ch. **xxiv**, sec. i, folio 4.

movement was instituted against him. In 12 A. D., realizing the discontent of the people, he issued a decree stating that, from then on, the imperial land and the private dependents could be bought and sold again without restriction. It was, however, too late for him to save the situation; his rule was doomed to complete failure.[1]

Unification of the Monetary System during the Latter Han Dynasty.—Wang Mang failed not only in the experiment of land nationalization by confiscation, but also in his attempt at a monetary reform. He abolished all the " ts'o-tao ", " ki-tao ", and " five tsu " coins of the preceding dynasty and made new coins of twenty-eight different denominations, employing such materials as gold, silver, tortoise shell, cowries, and copper. He called these " precious merchandise " (standard money) and " little money " (small denominations or subsidiary coins).[2] But the people did not approve of this new currency because the metals and other materials used were not pure and genuine. After a short time, they discarded it and began to employ again the " five tsu " coins of the Former Han dynasty. This was of course due to the fact that good money, *in the long run,* drove the bad money out of circulation. But another factor came into play in this instance—the loyalty of the people to the preceding dynasty and their refusal to acknowledge their new emperor who had murdered the former ruler and usurped the throne. This was proved when Wang Mang was mercilessly put to death in 23 A. D. and a descendant of the Han dynasty again took possession of the royal chair, renaming his House the " Latter Han dynasty."

[1] It should be pointed out, however, that, through the influence of the experiment of Wang Mang, partially if not entirely, the policy of abolishing slavery was tentatively put into effect during the reign of Emperor Kuang-wü of the Latter Han Dynasty (25-57 A. D.).

[2] Pan Ku, *History of Han*, ch. xxiv, sec. ii, folios 4-5.

Two years after the overthrow of Wang Mang, Ma Yuan, a scholar, statesman and successful military general of the time, advised the new emperor to have cast again the " five tsu " coins of the Former Han dynasty in order to unify the monetary system and get rid of the miscellaneous coins made by the government under Wang Mang, the value of which fluctuated violently, thereby throwing the market into confusion. His advice was eventually followed by the emperor. In 40 A. D., the " five tsu " coins were brought again into circulation, and a period of commercial prosperity followed.[1]

Centralization of the Auditing of Public Accounts during the Latter Han Dynasty.—Another important fiscal reform of the Latter Han dynasty was the publicity of accounts secured by requiring the officials in charge of the public accounts in each *chow* or province to make an annual report to the central government in person so that the latter might keep in constant touch with the administrative conditions in the various provinces and prefectures. The prefecture officers were held responsible to the provincial officers, while the latter were held in the same manner for any fraud or dishonesty found after the auditing of their accounts by the central government. This system had its origin far back in the Constitution of the Chou dynasty and was once employed by Emperor Wu of the Former Han dynasty, but it was best administered during the first part of the Latter Han dynasty. It contributed much to the promotion of administrative efficiency during that period, which is considered one of the brightest pages in Chinese political history.[2]

---

[1] *History of the Latter Han Dynasty*, ch. i, sec. ii, folio 3; ch. xxiv, folio 2. See also *History of Han*, ch. xxiv, sec. ii, folio 5.

[2] *Supplement to the History of the Latter Han Dynasty*, ch. xxviii, folio 1.

Reintroduction of the Tsing Tien System. — From the period of decay of the Latter Han dynasty to the reunification of the Chinese empire by the founder of the Tsin dynasty, China was for the most part in a state of turmoil caused by a series of civil wars which continued for about one hundred years. By 331 A. D. the population of the whole empire had been reduced to 16,163,863. The sparsity of inhabitants and the consequent desertion of landed property paved the way for the reintroduction of the *tsing tien* system by Emperor Wu, the founder of the Tsin dynasty.[1] This monarch was lacking in real statesmanship, as he did nothing for the maintenance of the system. Following his death, the whole nation was plunged again into disorder, and it was not until 477 A. D. that Emperor Hsiao-Wên of the Northern Wei dynasty succeeded in putting into effect the law of land equalization, which was regarded as a model by the statesmen of the Northern Ch'i, the Northern Chou, the Sui and the T'ang dynasties.[2]

The Abolition of the Salt Tax. — The founder of the Sui dynasty abolished the salt tax and followed the policy of levying taxes on land and families at the lowest possible rates. The period of his reign has been considered one of the most prosperous in Chinese history. Unfortunately, the son who succeeded this monarch was of quite different calibre. Through the frugality of the father, the son found the finances of the empire in a condition to permit whatever expenditure he saw fit to make. However, nothing is so easy as to exhaust the resources of a government by wastefulness or undue expansion of government works. Before long he had so depleted the treasury that he was forced to impose exorbitant taxes. These the people refused to bear

[1] *History of Tsin*, ch. xxvi.
[2] For a fuller account see Chen Huan-chang, *op. cit.*, pp. 510-516.

and the Suï dynasty came to an end with his death by assassi-
nation. The Chinese people, however, were, and are still,
indebted to this ruler for one great public improvement—
the Grand Canal system. This waterway, extending from
the northern to the southern part of the country, exercised a
great influence on the development of Southern China. Its
fiscal significance was marked: before the Sui dynasty, the
burden of taxation had fallen almost entirely on North China,
while after that time the southern provinces became fiscally
important, and contributed a larger share toward governmental revenue.[1]

*The Successful Administration of the System of Triple
Taxation during the Early Part of the T'ang Dynasty.*—
During the Tsin, Sui, and T'ang dynasties, what is known
as the triple tax system was developed. This system, modeled on the tax system of the Chou dynasty, provided for a
threefold levy, namely, a land tax, a labor tax, and a family
tax. In the early part of the Tsin dynasty, an equal distribution of land was made, and the land tax was merged with
the family tax, which was the main revenue of that period.
The reason for this was that each family was entitled to receive a certain amount of public land, and was therefore
required to pay a tax which was called a family tax. In the
Sui dynasty, we find the distinction between land revertible
to the government and land permanently possessed by the
family of the cultivator of the soil.

Although the growth of the triple tax system can be traced
in the fiscal history of the former dynasties, it was distinctly
a product of the T'ang period. The law, as finally proclaimed in 624 A. D., may be summarized as follows:

Among the recipients of public land, each adult male contributed annually two *shih*[2] of rice as a land tax. According to

[1] Feng, S. C., *Chapters on Chinese Fiscal History*, introduction.
[2] A *shih* was about 6.8 bushels.

the native products of its section, each household contributed as the family tax any one of the three kinds of silk—chuan, ling, and sh'ih—twenty *ch'ih* [1] in all and three *taels* [2] of floss-silk. If the household happened to be in a district or locality where there was no silk industry, it paid twenty-four ch'ih of cloth and three *catties* [3] of flax. The period of public service required of each man was twenty days a year. During a leap year, two days were added. A man who did not perform this service gave three *ch'ih* of silk in lieu of each day's work. Such a tax was called a labor tax. In some special cases, if fifteen additional days of service were given, the family tax was remitted; if thirty days were given, both the land and the family taxes were remitted. But, on the whole, the period of public service was not longer than fifty days. [4] In regard to the distribution of land, the same law provided that every man above eighteen years of age was entitled to receive one hundred *mou*; an aged or sick man, forty *mou*; a widow, thirty *mou*; if the latter was the head of a family twenty *mou* more were given to her. In all cases twenty *mou* of the land allotted were to remain the permanent possession of the family for the cultivation of mulberry, elm, date, or other trees which were suited to the land, while the rest was to revert to the government when the recipient died. [5]

Thus it is evident that under this system public ownership of land was supplemented by a certain amount of private ownership.

In the T'ang dynasty, as in the Chou dynasty, land was divided into three classes. In the case of land which was tillable only every other year, the individual was given twice the amount stated above; and in the case of that tillable only

[1] A *ch'ih* was about 14.1 inches.

[2] A *tael* was about 1/16 of a *catty*.

[3] A *catty* was about 21⅓ ounces avoirdupois.

[4] *Old History of T'ang*, ch. 48; *General Political History*, ch. 234; *General Research*, ch. ii.

[5] *New History of T'ang*, ch. 51, folio 1.

every third year, the grant per individual was three times as much. This rule was applied, however, only to the villages where land was sufficiently abundant to permit every cultivator to receive the full amount. In villages where there was not sufficient land, each was given the quota. If he wished to move to a village where there was an abundance of land, he might receive the full amount to which he was entitled.[1] The object of this provision was, of course, to equalize the distribution of the population in order to hasten the development of the backward districts.

In enforcing this threefold tax law, two important provisions were made. The first of these was that a general census should be taken every three years, and the families of each district divided into nine classes according to the extent of their property. A detailed record of the circumstances of each family was to be kept in the office of the local district where the family had its permanent residence, and copies of the record were to be sent to both the prefecture and the central government. The second provision was that each prefecture should submit to the central government an annual budget stating how much money was to be spent and how much to be raised; and that the amount of taxes to be collected must be made known to the public through notices posted by the local officers at definite places. Unless these two conditions were fulfilled, no one should be required to pay any tax.[2]

As a result of the weakening of the central government and the outbreak of a destructive rebellion which lasted more than twenty years, all the survey books and tax-rolls were destroyed, and the political conditions became precarious. At this critical moment, there came to the rescue a distinguished fiscal minister, Liu An, whose administration

[1] *New History of T'ang*, ch. 51, folio 1.
[2] *Old History of T'ang*, ch. 48, folio 2.

lasted from 760 to 780 A. D. and whose successful reform of the salt tax system established his reputation as a great financier, second only to Kuan Tzŭ.[1]

Reform of the Salt Tax Administration during the Middle Part of the T'ang Dynasty.—The reform in the administration of the salt tax made by Liu An was two-fold. First he combined government monopoly of the source of supply with free competition among the distributing agents. Formerly, the magistrates taxed the salt when the salt merchants transported it through any of their passes. Liu An made the salt industry a government monopoly, the officials buying salt from the people who produced it, and selling it to the merchants, who were allowed to transport it anywhere they wished without restriction and without paying any other exactions. Secondly, he controlled the supply of salt and kept its price at a constantly normal level. He accomplished this by transporting the government salt to those regions that were far removed from the salt-producing areas, and storing it there. When the salt merchants did not come to these areas with their wares, and the price of salt was high, he sold the reserve stock at a moderate price. He applied this principle to control the price level of rice also, because he thought that salt and rice were daily necessities of the people and that their prices should be kept as stable as possible. He called the former program the system of " constantly normal salt," and the latter that of " constantly normal grain." To insure the maintenance of a normal level in the price of rice, an average of three million *shih,* or Chinese bushels, was stored up in every prefecture. Through these measures the government reaped a considerable profit, while the people no longer suffered from excessive prices. As proof of the success of Liu An's administration of the salt monopoly, it

[1] *General Research,* ch. xv, folio 49.

is sufficient to mention that in the last one of his twenty years of service, more than one-half of the total revenue was derived from this monopoly alone. The profit secured was ten times that of the first year of his administration.

It is an indisputable fact that the strengthening of the central government in the middle part of the T'ang dynasty and its consequent restoration were largely due to the fiscal reforms of Liu An. The successful administration of this great financier was the result not only of his own genius, but of his wise choice of assistants. Sound character and good judgment, not mere skill and cleverness, were his criteria in choosing his administrative personnels. The caliber of the men he selected was demonstrated by the fact that after his death all of them proved themselves worthy of the offices to which they were appointed and of those to which they were promoted for their merit and success. He firmly believed that fiscal affairs should be entrusted to officials who had a sense of self-respect and valued principles more than expediency, and honor more than material gains.[1] A question of vital importance which presents itself today in China is whether the present Chinese fiscal administration has been placed in the hands of men of moral integrity and tested ability.

Fiscal Progress from the Middle of the T'ang Dynasty to the Latter Part of the Ming Dynasty (780-1580 A. D.)

In the period extending from the middle of the T'ang dynasty to the latter part of the Ming dynasty, the most noteworthy developments in the Chinese fiscal system were (1) the introduction of the semi-annual land tax system by Yang Yen, (2) the growth in importance of liquor and tea taxes, (3) the centralization of fiscal administration by the founder of the Sung dynasty, (4) the fiscal reforms of Wang An-shih during the middle of the Sung period, (5)

---

[1] *Old History of T'ang*, ch. 49, folio 2.

the rise of paper currency during the T'ang and Sung dynasties and its unprecedented inflation in the Yüan period, (6) the transitional changes of the land tax system and the public land policy during the period from the latter part of the T'ang dynasty to the beginning of the Ming dynasty, and (7) the reform of the salt tax administration during the "Five Dynasties," and the Sung, Yüan, and Ming dynasties.

Yang Yen's System of Semi-annual Land Taxation.—In the year 780, Yang Yen, then prime minister, introduced a plan of land taxation which became known as the semi-annual, or the " summer and autumn ", tax. This system is especially noteworthy in that its establishment brought to an end all attempts to revive the ancient system of *tsing tien*. Land nationalization, however, continued to be, and still is to a certain degree, a favorite topic of discussion among Confucian theorists.

The system of Yang Yen was outlined by the author as follows:

All families, whether native or from another administrative district, shall be registered according to their present residence. All persons, minors as well as adults, shall be classified according to their wealth. A land tax shall be collected twice a year, in the summer and the autumn, but those who find it more convenient may make payment in three instalments. All other taxes shall be abolished, but a fixed amount shall be added to the land tax in lieu of the poll tax levied hitherto. Those who have no fixed residence and are engaged in trade shall be required to pay an annual tax amounting to one-thirtieth of their profits, in order that they may bear the burden of taxation equally with the farmers. The acreage of land under cultivation, as assessed and recorded in the year 779 A. D., shall be used as a standard for levying the land tax hereafter. The administration of the tax system shall be placed in the hands of an official to be known as the commissioner of bi-annual land taxation. Collectors for the various districts shall be appointed by the central government. These officers shall be empowered to exempt from taxation persons who are unable to make payments. Officials levying taxes at a higher rate than the one prescribed by the government shall be punished by law. Above all, the annual income of the government should be regulated by its annual expenditure, and therefore an estimate of national expenditure should first be made every year, and the required amount of land tax be apportioned among the various tax districts according to their acreage of cultivated land.[1]

It will be seen that this system embodied a number of important fiscal reforms, the chief among which were (a) the simplification of the tax system through the abolition of all direct taxes other than the land and poll taxes, and the incorporation of these into one tax; (b) the change of the taxation basis from person or family to property and income; (c) the practical application of the principles of equality and universality of taxation, exemplified by the placing of a tax on business profits as well as on agricultural profits; (d) the provision of tax exemption for those unable to pay, but not for persons of means such as the priests or the families of government officials who had hitherto enjoyed freedom from taxation; (e) the substitution of money payment for the personal service and family taxes; (f) the regulation of government revenue by expenditure instead of the regulation of the expenditure by the revenue as was formerly done, and (g) the adoption of the apportionment system in the field of land taxation instead of the fixed percentage system which China had hitherto employed.

All the changes made by Yang Yen were severely attacked by his contemporary conservative statesmen led by Lu Chih, a great Confucian statesman of the T'ang period, whose criticism of the new system ran as follows:

The production of wealth depends upon the labor of men.

[1] *General Research*, ch. iii, folio 15.

Therefore, when the ancient wise rulers regulated taxation, they took the person as the basis. . . . Recognizing this fundamental principle of taxation, the founder of the present dynasty divided taxes into three main classes—land tax, family tax, and personal service tax, which were levied respectively on the produce of land, the products of a household, and the physical labor of an adult. This system had been successfully administered for more than a century following the establishment of the dynasty. It was only after the outbreak of the disastrous rebellion that it gave way, owing to the excessive demands upon it for the maintenance of numerous standing armies and because of the loss of records which were essential to the equitable distribution of land and population. The failure was due not to the collapse of the fiscal structure, but to the temporary political disorganization.

Now, the semi-annual land tax system takes property, not the person, as its basis. It also takes the year of maximum revenue, i. e., the year 779 A. D., as its standard. The former principle is contrary to the generally accepted economic doctrine that labor is the sole source of social wealth, while the latter is simply a combination of numerous excessive illegal taxes as a permanent system, if it is worth the name system. Moreover, among the various kinds of property, some are small in quantity, and yet high in value; some are bulky in magnitude, but worth little. Some can be easily hidden from view, while others must be stored in gardens or granaries. Some are used for productive purposes, whereas others, such as buildings and household furnishings are employed chiefly for consumption. Inasmuch as the semi-annual tax system lays much emphasis on landed property, less on business profits, and leaves the personal property untouched, the inevitable result will be that those who acquire personal property and move about will usually escape taxes, while those who pursue agriculture and establish a permanent home will always have to pay. Such a system encourages the people to commit fraud and is bound to result in a grave inequality in the distribution of taxation.[1]

[1] *Old History of T'ang*, ch. 52, folios 1-2; *General Research*, ch. iii, folio 16.

There was a certain amount of justice in this criticism. The evils of the semi-annual land tax were much the same as those of a general property tax in modern times. Lu Chih, however, failed to see that Yang Yen's system was devised to meet three important needs of the time: (1) the restoration of the government's taxing power which was shattered by the twenty years' internal warfare; (2) the adoption of a fiscal program taking into account the free movement of population, which had followed the abolition of the public-land system; and (3) the prevention of the evasion by the wealthy class of the general landed property tax, a problem apparently even more important than that of preventing the evasion of the personal property tax. Therefore, although Yang Yen's system of semi-annual land taxation had its shortcomings, it met certain vital problems and played an important part in the development of land taxation in China.

The Growth in Importance of the Liquor Tax.—The history of the liquor tax in China is full of interest. As early as 2205 B. C., at the beginning of the Hsia dynasty, an order prohibiting the manufacture and consumption of expensive and intoxicating liquors was proclaimed. In the reign of Emperor Wu of the Former Han dynasty a system of liquor monopoly was instituted. As the result of a strong protest from Confucian leaders, this monopoly was converted into a form of taxation on the profits of liquor business, and the maximum price of liquor was limited by law to four cash a *sheng,* i. e., 1.095 quarts. During the rule of Wang Mang, the monopoly system was restored, but as his régime was shortlived, this was soon abolished again. Then a new prohibition law was put into effect which lasted throughout the Latter Han dynasty. This law, however, differed from the old prohibition law in that the former was devised to eliminate the waste of foodstuffs in the manufacture of liquors and was introduced as a necessary measure for the relief and prevention of famine, while the latter was based primarily on the proposition that liquor consumption is morally undesirable.

For a time systems of liquor monopoly and liquor taxation alternated with one another, sometimes in rapid succession. At the beginning of the Sui dynasty, the liquor tax was abolished along with the salt tax, and liquor manufacture was made an open industry; but in the latter part of the T'ang dynasty, the heavy demands on the central government created by military exigencies necessitated a revival of the liquor tax. Three methods were put into operation one after the other during this period: (1) taxation on the net profits of all liquor businesses, (2) taxation in the form of license fees, which were exacted at three different rates according to the business standing of the dealer; and (3) taxation on brewers' yeast. Thus liquor became one of the principal objects of taxation, whether the tax was based on business profits, on the privilege of license, on consumption, or on the raw material for production. At that time, however, the administration of the tax was far from successful owing to the political disturbance of the empire and to the evasion of taxation because of its excessively high rate.[1]

Development of the Tea Tax.—In the year 780 A. D., a tax of ten per cent on the production of tea was introduced as a war measure. Two years later, when the emergency had passed, this law was repealed; but it was reintroduced in 793 to supplement the revenue from the land tax, which had fallen below normal because of flood devastations. The revenue from the tea tax grew steadily, for the popularity of tea greatly increased in social circles after a noted scholar of the time, Lu Yü, strongly recommended its use in his well-known book called *The Tea Classic.*[2]

[1] *General Research*, ch. xviii, folio 64.
[2] *Ibid.*, ch. xvii, folios 58-60.

In 821, the rate of the tea tax was raised to fifteen per cent in order to meet the needs of the central government. This policy was severely criticized by Li Chia, a Confucian states-man of the time, on the following grounds: (1) that tea was first taxed as an emergency measure in a time of military stress, and that, as the rate of taxation then had been only ten per cent *ad valorem,* it would be unjustifiable to raise this rate in time of peace; (2) that tea is a beverage necessary to the general public, and that the high price which would undoubtedly result from the imposition of a heavy tax on its production would deprive the ordinary people of its use and seriously incommode them; and (3) that the increasing demand for tea would greatly stimulate its production, and that the revenue of the government would be augmented by the increase of its production, but that this development would inevitably be checked to a great extent if the rate of the tax were raised to fifteen per cent.[1] The protest of Li Chia was unheeded however. And, furthermore, certain illegal exactions such as local transit duties and exorbitant storage rates were imposed on the tea merchants by the government. Early in 847, a reform was made in the tax in the direction of eliminating all the illegal taxes and only licensed mer-chants were thereafter allowed to engage in the tea trade. As a result, the revenue from this source was soon more than double that of the year 793.[1]

The Centralization of the Fiscal Administration by the Founder of the Sung Dynasty.—Before we proceed to dis-cuss the various policies adopted by the founder of the Sung dynasty for the fiscal organization of the empire, a few words about the political situation prior to the establishment of this dynasty are deemed necessary. During the latter part of the T'ang dynasty, a régime of military despotism

[1] *New History of T'ang,* ch. 54, folio 2.

existed. Toward the end of the dynasty the military governors usurped the power of taxation from the central government and kept possession of the bulk of the collected funds under the names of " revenues retained for the local district " and " revenues retained for the military governors." According to a fiscal report made by the famous premier Li Chi-fu in 808, only eight provinces out of fifteen were at that time sending any part of their annual revenue to the central government. The households of the country then totaled 1,440,000, only one-fourth of the number recorded in 754,[1] while the standing army numbered 830,000, an increase of more than one-third over the national enlistment of the year 742. The ratio between the national income and the amount spent for the maintenance of officers, soldiers, merchants and priests was defined as follows: " It requires two households to support a soldier, and three farmers to provide for seven more or less idle consumers." [2]

From this time on, the cost of maintaining the army steadily increased, and the fiscal conditions grew worse. The total annual revenue derived from land, liquor, salt and tea taxes amounted to only 9,220,000 strings of cash. The sole resort in this extremity was to collect in advance the land tax of the next year, and then that of the year following.

Under this régime the central government became so weak and unstable that emperors were usually made or unmade by a set of eunuchs backed by the military commanders. In turn, these commanders were made or unmade by their subordinates with or even without the nominal assent of the central government. The policies which the statesmen of the time advocated as remedies for these evils were: (a) the subdivision of the former military districts into smaller units, so that the commanders in the various districts might

[1] The household was at that time the unit of population census.

[2] *General Research*, ch. xxiii, folio 36.

have more limited powers and less prestige, (b) the centralization of the military administration, so that the semifeudal military commanders could be dismissed at the discretion of the imperial government, and (c) the replacement of the military commanders dismissed by the central government or overthrown by their own subordinates with carefully chosen civilian officials in order that the military affairs might be brought under the control of the civil administration. Unfortunately, these policies were never put through with success; and consequently the T'ang Empire was broken up into a number of petty independent kingdoms, the more noted ones of which were commonly known as the " Five Dynasties." [1] After the lapse of fifty years, these kingdoms were again united by Chao K'uang-yin, the founder of the Sung dynasty.[2]

With the birth of this dynasty, the military autocracy came to an end. The new emperor, fearful lest the " Imperial Yellow Robe," given to him by his comrade militarists, be some day taken from him at their discretion, determined to break the power of these military leaders. He gathered the various commanders together at a banquet and informed them that he proposed appointing them military governors in the outside districts. He hinted that they were expected to resign their commands in the imperial army stationed in the capital before they accepted their new posts, because henceforth the military affairs were to be placed under the control of a privy council, which was to be comprised of civilians instead of soldiers. To this plan of the new emperor all of the military commanders pledged their full support, and he thus achieved his first success in

[1] These "Five Dynasties" were Posterior Liang (907–923 A. D.), Posterior T'ang (923–936), Posterior Tsin (936–947), Posterior Han (947–951), and Posterior Chou (951–960).

[2] Y. C. Li, *Li Wei-kung, the Statesman*, pp. 61-82.

centralizing military administration and doing away with the military magnates.

At the present time the Chinese people as a whole are experiencing an uneasiness similar to that under which Chao K'uang-yin suffered. The so-called military governors of today are trying to rob the Chinese people of their right to elect their president by forcing the resignation of men raised to the presidency by popular choice and substituting officials of their own selection, whom they may depose if their selfish ambitions so dictate. These tactics differ very little in essence from those of the military commanders of the latter part of the T'ang dynasty and of the " Five Dynasties." And the corrupt practices through which the worthless politicians of the present day are ruining their nation are surprisingly analogous to the methods by which the eunuchs of the T'ang period brought about the collapse of a great empire.

A lesson that may be learned from the founder of the Sung dynasty is that military reform and house-cleaning in the administrative departments are two prerequisites to the political and fiscal reorganization of a nation. After effecting the centralization of military administration, he lost no time in depriving the military commanders of their traditional fiscal powers. He appointed imperial agents to collect taxes in the various districts of his empire, and he restrained the military governors and the civil magistrates from holding offices in these districts and from interference in fiscal matters. Therefore the fiscal officers were unhampered in the execution of their duties. They were appointed by the central government, held responsible to the emperor for the collection of taxes, and required to make their reports direct to him.

Fiscal Reforms of Wang An-shih during the Middle of the Sung Period. — The military centralization effected by the founder of the Sung dynasty had its merits, but it had also its deficiencies. It did away with the evils of military despotism, but it weakened the military force necessary for national defence, and China became a prey of the warlike northern tribes. When, about the middle of the Northern Sung dynasty, the country was threatened with invasion by the Khitans, one of the strongest of these tribes, Premier Wang An-shih formulated two plans for the improvement of the army: one, called the Militia Act, was a system of tithing for police as well as military purposes; the other was a system of guaranteeing the army a sufficient supply of cavalry horses for use in case of war. In order to put these military reforms into effect Wang An-shih introduced four measures for the reorganization of the national fiscal system: (a) the Farm Loan Act, (b) a system of government produce exchange, (c) the abolition of corvée and the establishment of a general property tax, and (d) the reorganization of the fiscal administration.

The Farm Loan Act of 1069 A. D. — Recognizing that the military strength of the Chinese nation depended on its economic strength, and that the agricultural peoples constituted the bulk of the whole population of the country, Wang An-shih first turned his attention to the betterment of the conditions of the farmer. In addition to the enactment of measures for the irrigation and improvement of agricultural lands and for the equalization of land taxes, he proclaimed a farm-loan act in 1069. This law was originally called the "system of green-sprout money" because its purpose was to lend money to needy farmers when their grain crop was only in the green-sprout stage. The duration of the loan was short; the money lent in the first month of the year was to be repaid in the summer from the crop of the land, while that lent in the fifth month was to be paid in the autumn. If the crop was bad, the farmer was allowed to return the money at the next harvest season. The rate of interest charged was twenty per cent. This system had worked well in a district of Ningpo when Wang An-shih had held the office of magistrate there. Unfortunately its nation-wide application was not so successful. The officers misunderstood the purpose of its originator: they tried in so far as possible to lend money to the rich farmers, since such investment of the government funds was much safer than loans to the poor, which might not be repaid and would make a bad showing on official records.

The farm-loan act met with bitter criticism and opposition from those who believed that the state should not engage in the business of banking. Wang An-shih contended, however, that since the rate of interest charged on loans by the private capitalists of the time was over fifty per cent, agricultural banking on the part of the government was an absolute necessity. He pointed out that, as the farm-loan act allowed repayment in grain if the borrower found this more convenient, and made provision for deferred payment when crops were bad, the twenty per cent interest which it permitted the government to charge included such expenses as fees for transportation, storage, and insurance against the possible failure and bankruptcy of the borrower. This was a strong argument on the part of Wang An-shih, but he followed an unwise policy in charging a uniform rate of interest on loans instead of making separate charges for storage and other services.

Another criticism directed against the law was that it fostered favoritism by vesting in local officials the power to decide whether or not a farmer's crop was sufficiently poor to warrant an extension of time on his loan. Eventually this favoritism became so flagrant that the farm-loan act fell into discredit with the general public, and it was abolished when Wang An-shih resigned the premiership. But with the return to power of his disciples, it was revived with the following modifications: (a) the annual rate of interest was reduced to ten per cent, (b) the amount of the loans to be made each year was no longer fixed, (c) officials were for-bidden to force loans upon the people, and (d) no special reward was to be given to officials who made good personal records by lending money to the rich through a system of forced apportionment. This new policy remained in effect until the fall of the Northern Sung dynasty in 1126 A. D.[1]

The System of Government Produce Exchange.—Follow-ing the models of the government banking system of the Chou dynasty and the level-standard system of the Former Han dynasty, Wang An-shih in 1072 established an insti-tute of government exchange. Its functions were of four kinds, namely, that of a loan bank, that of a produce ex-change, that of a market place and that of a central organ-ization for the purchase of general governmental supplies. The purpose of the institute was to enable the government to adjust the supply of commodities to the current demands and thus prevent the merchant class from exploiting either the consumer or the producer. The chief difference between this system and that of farm loans was that the latter was a type of agricultural banking, whereas the former was a system of public produce exchange coupled with a form of commercial banking.

The produce-exchange system was first put into operation in an outlying city in 1070 as a supplementary measure of national defence and an aid to frontier development. After two years' successful experiment, a central governmental produce exchange was established in the capital, and a num-ber of branches were started in the leading cities of the country. The members of the various mercantile guilds

[1] *History of Sung,* ch. 176, folios 4-8.

were eligible to membership in the exchange. Merchants were required to join the exchange in groups of five, each member of a group guaranteeing the liabilities of the other members.

By furnishing a surety of four persons, or a pledge of real estate or silver or gold bullion, individual citizens were allowed to borrow money from the exchange or to buy government commodities according to the value of their pledge. Interest was charged at the rate of twenty per cent a year. The exchange was permitted to purchase at a reasonable price goods for which the producers could find no market at the time; when a demand for these commodities arose, the exchange was obligated to sell them at a moderate price without attempting to reap special profits. When the various departments of the government were in need of anything, they were required to buy it from the exchange.

Thus it may be seen that Wang An-shih aspired to cover with his program not only the fields of commercial banking and produce exchange, but also those of frontier development, national preparedness, and governmental economy through the direct purchase of the general supplies from the central and local commodity exchanges. His exchange system, however, did not meet with prolonged success. Most of the small merchants did not wish to become members of the agency, preferring to remain free of its arbitrary power and to sell their goods independently. They therefore avoided the localities where government exchanges were in operation. As a result the profits derived from the exchanges were not sufficient to counterbalance the loss of the commodity taxes which were formerly imposed. In some cases, the receipts were too meagre to cover expenses. In the year 1128 the exchange finally passed out of existence.[1]

---

[1] *History of Sung*, ch. 186, folios 3-4.

The Abolition of the Corvée and the Establishment of a General Property Tax. — In the year 1070 Wang An-shih issued a mandate abolishing the corvée or personal service tax, and substituting for this a general property tax, to be paid by each family in money and at a rate to be determined in accordance with its wealth. There were three forms of this tax, viz., the *commutation tax,* which was to be paid by those who were formerly required to serve in public offices as tax-collectors, messengers, policemen, or transportation personnel; the *commutation aid,* which was to be paid by the families of officials, and by monks, widows and orphaned only sons, who were formerly exempted from the payment of the personal-service tax; and the *contribution for the commutation reserve fund,* which was to be raised by an extra assessment at the rate of twenty per cent on those who were required to pay either of the two former taxes and which was designed to provide a reserve against such emergencies as years of famine or inundations in which the people might be unable to pay their taxes.

The commutation of enforced labor was strongly attacked by the aristocratic element because it forced this class to pay an additional tax in order to lighten the burden of the lower classes, while persons of small means were exempt from the exaction. And many of the conservative statesmen fought against the reform, maintaining that the social distinction between the upper and lower classes was insuperable and that it was more convenient for the lower classes to pay their corvées in labor than in money. They based their arguments on the proposition that labor is a form of personal wealth possessed by every able-bodied individual, and that in exchanging labor or the product of labor for money the individual usually suffers a loss. As a result, although the change was successfully put into effect for a time, the system of corvée was reinstated again in 1086.[1]

---

[1] *History of Sung,* ch. 177, folios 1-7; ch. 178, folios 1-5.

The Reform of the Fiscal Administration.—When Wang An-shih came into power in 1069, one of his first undertakings was the reorganization of the fiscal administration.[1] At that time, the Department of Public Economy, which consisted of three bureaus, namely, the Bureau of Estimates and Expenditures, the Bureau of Salt and Iron Taxes, and the Bureau of Population and Land Taxation, was independent of the Cabinet and the Privy Council. The defect of this scheme of organization was that the Cabinet controlled the civil affairs, the Privy Council, the military affairs, the Department of Public Economy, the fiscal affairs, and there was no central organization above these offices except the Crown. The original purpose of the arrangement had been to establish a system of checks and balances among these three main administrative bodies, and to secure to the emperor the reins of the government. But the system was one that would work satisfactorily only under a good and capable emperor. Wang An-shih saw this clearly. He therefore proposed to establish an office in which were to be vested the powers of prime minister, minister of public economy, and minister of economic development and social welfare. This plan met with the approval of the emperor, and it was put into effect with conspicuous success. Wang An-shih defined the functions of the new office in such terms as to check and control the influence of private capitalists, to protect and help the poorer classes, to develop the national resources, to keep the various forms of money in constant circulation, and to maintain the government finances in sound condition without resort to steady increase in taxation. He succeeded in stopping the wasteful expenditures of the government by the rigid application of budgetary procedures. Within a short period government disbursements

[1] *General Research,* ch. 24, folios 39-41; see also, Liang Chi-ch'ao, *Wang An-shih, the Statesman,* pp. 92-97.

were reduced to sixty per cent of the preceding budget. In other words, Wang An-shih made a cut of forty per cent in the national expenditure by simply eliminating wasteful and unnecessary outlays.

The government accounting system of the Sung dynasty has long been regarded as the most elaborate accounting procedure employed during the imperial period of Chinese fiscal history. In 1072 a Bureau of Accounts was created under the auspices of the prime minister and the minister of public economy for the examination of accounts submitted by the various departments of the central government and by the provincial administrative offices. Two years later, a reform was made in governmental accounting and a uniform system of reporting was introduced which would permit a comparison of the various items of revenue and expenditure from year to year.[1]

The fiscal system of Wang An-shih broke down before the Northern Sung period came to a close and his name was listed among the despised radicals. It is needless to say that after the failure of his tremendous political and economic experiments the conservative Chinese scholars again came to the fore and the development of fiscal study witnessed another setback. The reforms of this distinguished statesman, however, have had a lasting influence on Chinese fiscal thought, and he has been accorded a place among the great leaders of the country. Since 1900 recognition of his work has been especially widespread.

The Rise of Paper Currency and its Inflation during the Sung, Kin and Yüan Dynasties.—The story of the development of paper currency in China is a long one. Its early beginnings may be traced in the *li pu,* or cloth currency, of

[1] For an account of the development of the government accounting system during the Sung dynasty, see *History of Sung,* ch. 179, folios 1-7.

the Chou dynasty and the *pê lu p'i,* or leather currency, employed in the time of Emperor Han Wu. In the year 812 A. D., during the reign of Emperor Hsien-tsung of the T'ang dynasty the government issued bills of domestic exchange, or, as they were popularly called, " flying money," for the purpose of meeting the scarcity of copper coins, which presented itself as a most serious monetary problem at that time.[1]

The flying money of the T'ang dynasty has long been considered as a form of paper currency because of the fact that a large volume of business was done by means of this substitute for metallic money. It lacked, however, at least one of the essential characteristics of paper currency in that it was issued upon the demand of the remitter in such amounts as he wished, and was therefore not of fixed denominations like the paper money devised in later times for the use of the general public and for the purpose of general circulation.

When the first emperor of the Sung dynasty came to the throne in 960, he continued the practice of issuing governmental bills of exchange. In 970 he created an office known as the Convenient Money Service for conducting the business of exchange. In 997, the amount of money represented by the bills of exchange issued was 1,700,000 strings of cash. Twenty years later, it had risen to 2,930,000 strings.[2]

It was not until 1005 that a real system of paper currency came into use.[3] This currency consisted of notes which were called " evidences of money credit," and was first employed in the province of Szechuan, where heavy and

[1] *History of T'ang,* ch. 54, folio 4.

[2] *History of Sung,* ch. 180, folio 3.

[3] For the development of paper currency in its relation to the invention of paper and printing, see T. F. Carter, *The Invention of Printing in China and Its Spread Westward,* Columbia University Press, 1925, pp. 70-81.

inconvenient iron money had been used in commercial transactions. The evidences of money credit were issued by a
banking organization consisting of sixteen leading rich
families of the province, and as these notes were redeemable
once in three years, they were given the name of *kiao-tzŭ*,
or redeemable notes. In 1023 the banking organization was
dissolved on account of its failure to meet obligations, and
consequently the business of note-issue was taken over by
the government. A limit for the amount of issue was set
at 1,256,340 notes, each of which represented 1,000 copper
coins.[1] Strictly speaking, this form of government notes,
redeemable only at definite periods, should be designated as
circulating redeemable bonds or non-interest-bearing treasury
notes rather than paper money. But the name paper money
has always been applied to the notes for the reason that they
were issued by the government, not for the purpose of making loans, but for the convenience of the general public as a
substitute for money.

Toward the end of the eleventh century, the currency system of the Sung dynasty began to break down. Government
notes were issued far beyond the legal limit; the reserve
fund for their redemption was exhausted; and, worst of all,
enormous numbers of new notes were put out in the form
of old notes in order that the public might be kept in ignor-
ance of the excessive over-issue that was taking place. The
last-mentioned measure, which was resorted to in the year
1107, was little more than an unlawful means of government
borrowing through illegal note-issue. As a result of this
extreme inflation of the currency, a note representing one
thousand cash came to be worth only a little more than ten
cash.[2]

At the close of the Sung régime several other forms of

---

[1] *History of Sung*, ch. ix, folio 1; ch. 181, folio 1.
[2] *Ibid.*, ch. 181, folio 1.

government notes were issued. The policy followed amounted
to nothing more than the issue of new notes in order to re-
deem the old notes; and, as a matter of fact, no cash redemption was made at all. In 1247, it was declared that
two issues of government notes should hereafter be kept in
permanent circulation, and thus notes redeemable in name
were made irredeemable in practice.[1]

In the Kin dynasty (1115 to 1134 A. D.), two regulations
were adopted which are worthy of mention: one was that
the government notes should continue to circulate as long
as they were in good condition; the other was that their
circulation should be made universal throughout the country
irrespective of provincial boundaries, which had hitherto
caused much hindrance to the popular use of paper currency.
But the inflation of paper money during the last years of
this dynasty was even greater than that which had occurred
in the Sung dynasty. It was said that a bundle of 10,000
paper notes would purchase no more than a single piece of
bread.[2]

The unsound system of paper currency brought the Sung
and the Kin dynasties to an end. The amount of paper currency issued under these régimes became dwarfed, however,
when compared with that issued by the ensuing Yüan government. The history of the Yüan régime may be divided
into five periods:

(i) The period from 1237 to 1259, in which the policy
of a limited issue of paper currency was adopted. The
amount of the first issue was fixed at 10,000 *tings,* representing 50,000 taels of silver.[3]

---

[1] *History of Sung,* ch. 181, folios 1-3.

[2] *History of Kin,* ch. 48, especially folio 6. See also *History of Yüan,*
ch. 146, folio 3.

[3] *History of Yüan,* ch. 146, folio 2. See also Cordier, H., *Histoire
Générale de la Chine,* vol. ii, p. 240.

(ii) The period from 1260 to 1287, in which the *Chung-t'ung* notes [1] were issued annually in the following amounts:

Year	Amount	Year	Amount	Year	Amount
1260	73,352	1270	96,768	1280	1,135,800
1261	39,139	1271	47,000	1281	1,094,800 [3]
1262	80,000	1272	86,256	1282	969,444 [3]
1263	74,000 [2]	1273	110,192	1283	610,620
1264	89,208 [2]	1274	247,440	1284	629,904
1265	116,208	1275	398,194	1285	2,043,080 [5]
1266	77,252	1276	1,419,665	1286	2,181,600
1267	109,488	1277	1,021,645	1287	83,200
1268	29,880	1278	1,023,400		
1269	22,896 [2]	1279	788,320		

(iii) The period from 1287 to 1309, in which the *Chih-yüan* notes were issued annually in the following amounts:

Year	Amount	Year	Amount	Year	Amount
1287	1,001,017	1295	310,000	1303	1,500,000
1288	921,612	1296	400,000	1304	500,000
1289	1,780,093	1297	400,000	1305	500,000
1290	500,250	1298	299,910	1306	1,000,000
1291	500,000	1299	900,075	1307	1,000,000
1292	500,000	1300	600,000	1308	1,000,000
1293	260,000	1301	500,000	1309	1,000,000
1294	193,706	1302	2,000,000		

(iv) The period from 1310 to 1311, in which 1,450,368 *tings* of *Chih-ta* silver notes were issued.

[1] *Chung-t'ung* and *Chih-yüan* were the two periods into which the reign of Emperor Kuplai was divided. The Chung-t'ung period extended from 1260 to 1263, and the Chih-yüan period from 1264 to 1294. But the notes bearing these names were issued even in the reigns of his successors.

[2] These three numbers were misprinted as 46,000; 89,280; and 22,886 *tings* respectively in J. Edkins, *Banking and Prices in China*, 1905, p. 230.

[3] These five issues were left out in Edkins's book and in H. B. Morse's table showing the amount of paper currency existing in the Yüan dynasty, as appeared in his article on Chinese Currency in the *Journal of the Royal Asiatic Society, North China Branch*, 1907, vol. 38, p. 23.

[4] All these issues were in terms of a *ting*, which legally represented five *taels* of silver.

[5] Chih-ta was the name of the reign of Emperor Wu of the Yüan dynasty.

(v) The period from 1311 to 1330, in which both the *Chih-yüan* and the *Chung-t'ung* notes were issued annually except in the year 1328 when no notes were put out on account of political disturbances. The amounts of each year's issue were as follows:

Year	Chih-yüan	Chung-t'ung
1311	2,150,000 tings	150,000 tings
1312	2,222,336 "	100,000 "
1313	2,000,000 "	200,000 "
1314	2,000,000 "	100,000 "
1315	1,000,000 "	100,000 "
1316	400,000 "	100,000 "
1317	480,000 "	100,000 "
1318	400,000 "	100,000 "
1319	1,480,000 "	100,000 "
1320	1,480,000 "	100,000 "
1321	1,000,000 "	50,000 "
1322	800,000 "	50,000 "
1323	700,000 "	50,000 "
1324	600,000 "	150,000 "
1325	400,000 "	100,000 "
1326	400,000 "	100,000 "
1327	400,000 "	100,000 "
1329	310,920 "	30,500 "
1330	1,192,000 "	40,000 "

It will be seen that throughout the period from 1260 to 1330—a period of seventy years—there was issued a comparatively small quantity of silver notes.[1] The other two kinds of paper notes, *Chung-t'ung* and *Chih-yüan,* were practically irredeemable. The *Chih-ta* silver notes were withdrawn from circulation on the ground that the ratio fixed for the exchange between the new form of notes and the other two older forms of notes was not an appropriate one. Although the depreciation of *Chung-t'ung* and *Chih-yüan* notes was exceedingly great, that did not justify the legal ratio of one silver note to five *Chih-yüan* notes or

[1] *History of Yüan, ch. 93,* folios 6-7.

twenty-five *Chung-t'ung* notes as was then fixed by the government. It was also arbitrarily determined by law that a silver note was to be exchangeable for one tael of silver or one ounce of gold, and that private dealings in gold and silver were to be thereafter prohibited. All these regulations were found impracticable after eighteen months' experiment, and no further attempt at monetary reform was made in this direction. Instead, the issuing of both the *Chih-yüan* and the *Chung-t'ung* notes was continued, the former serving as the higher denomination and the latter as the lower denomination. Toward the end of the Yüan régime, the market was flooded with exceedingly depreciated paper currency, much of which was counterfeit despite the heavy punishment meted out to counterfeiters.[1]

Another point which should be mentioned in this connection is that throughout its entire rule the Yüan government minted no copper coins except in the year 1310, when a government minting office was created and copper cash were coined. But that office was abolished in the following year together with silver currency notes.[2]

The explanation of this development of a monetary system based almost entirely upon paper currency was that the Mongol government, instead of keeping gold and silver as a reserve fund for the redemption of notes issued, lavishly employed them as gifts to the members of the imperial family, to victorious generals, and to civil officers in recognition of their dignity or their merits. The matter of annual donations to the members of the imperial family and to distinguished officers occupied so conspicuous and so important a place in public finance that the writer of the *History of Yüan* devoted one of his special chapters on fiscal subjects to the regulations governing these annual gifts.[3] The statesman

[1] *History of Yüan*, ch. 97, folio 1, sec. ii.

[2] *Ibid.*, ch. 93, folio 3, sec. vi; also ch. 97, folio 1, sec. ii.

[3] *Ibid.*, ch. 95, folios 1-10.

who advocated the policy of limited note-issue in 1237 and warned against the evil consequences of the inflation of paper currency long before these manifested themselves, was Yali Chu-ts'ai. He cited the downfall. of the Kin dynasty through its over-issue of paper currency as a lesson which the government officers, especially those in charge of currency administration, should bear in mind.[1] Unfortunately, his advice was unheeded by his successors.

Transitional Changes of the Land Tax System and the Public Land Policy during the Period from the Latter Part of the T'ang Dynasty to the Beginning of the Ming Dynasty. —During the latter half of the T'ang dynasty and throughout the subsequent " Five Dynasties " (907-960 A. D.), we find no sign of progress in the system of land taxation. On the contrary, the semi-annual land tax system of Yang Yen broke down rapidly, and the raising of the rate, and the collecting of the land taxes before they became due were prevalent practices. In 924, an office called the Board of Land and Personal Service Taxes was established by the Posterior T'ang dynasty. But owing to the political disturbance of the time no fiscal order was possible.[2]

After the reunification of the empire by the first emperor of the Sung dynasty, the revenue system consisted of five kinds of taxes, viz., rent collected from the public lands placed under private cultivation, taxes on private land holdings, house and land taxes in the municipalities, poll and personal-service taxes and commodity taxes. At the beginning of this new régime the policy of light taxation was strictly followed. Sometimes land was taxed at the rate of one-twentieth, sometimes one-thirtieth, of its yield. In some extreme cases, four out of every hundred *mou* were taxed

[1] *History of Yüan*, ch. 146, folio 3.
[2] *General Research*, ch. iii, folios 18-20.

at the lowest possible rate. The taxing of twenty *mou* out of every hundred was still considered exorbitant.[1]

The assessment of land for the purpose of levying land taxes was rather strictly enforced in the early part of the Sung dynasty. Local administrators in charge of this function who failed to do their duty were severely punished. But the declaration of acreage by the owners themselves gradually supplanted actual survey, and arrears in payment of land taxes were cancelled in years of famine. Both of these practices gave opportunity for dishonesty, fraud and inequality in the distribution of the burden of land taxation. In the year 1142 a survey of the land in the province of Chekiang and in some districts of the province of Fukien was made. However, when Chu Hsi, a great Confucian statesman of the time, sought to apply the same policy in the Ting, Chang, and Chien prefectures of Fukien province, the large landowners, who under-declared the amount of their holdings and thus evaded the payment of taxation, employed every means to oppose him, and his policy was finally obstructed in spite of the fact that the, weaker members of society were anxious to have the land tax evenly redistributed.[2] We may therefore say that throughout the whole course of the Sung dynasty, nation-wide land assessment was never satisfactorily accomplished.

One reform in the administration of land taxation was achieved, however, during this dynasty. Although the general plan for the collection of land taxes was still along the line of the semi-annual system of Yang Yen, the Sung government went a step further. Instead of laying down a definite period for the collection of the taxes throughout the country, the time was set in the various localities in accordance with the season of harvest. For instance, in the

[1] *History of Sung*, ch. 174, folios 1-3.
[2] *History of Sung*, ch. 173, folio 6.

districts of the imperial domain, the collection of the summer tax began on the fifteenth day of the fifth month and ended on the thirtieth day of the seventh month; whereas, in the districts of the Ho-pei and Ho-tung provinces, where the harvest season was later, the collection began on the same date, but was not terminated until the fifth day of the eighth month.[1] The changes made in later times to permit extension of the period of collection in certain districts were based on the same principle.

An attempt at the disposal of public land during this period is also noteworthy. In 996 all such land was given out to the people for cultivation, free of charge and exempt from taxation for the first five years. The amount given to each family of less than three adults was 100, 150, or 200 *mou* according to the quality of the land. For a time the capital necessary for cultivating the land was lent by the government, but this policy was soon discontinued on account of lack of funds.

In the year 1263, a vicious fiscal policy was put into operation, namely, the buying up of private land by the government with depreciated paper money issued for the purpose. From the produce of land thus brought under its control the government expected to add considerably to its revenue. But its bad faith and maladministration lost it the support of the people at large, and the Sung empire came to an end in the year 1276.[2]

When the Yüan dynasty came into power, the tax system applied in China Proper was in some respects a combination

---

[1] *History of Sung*, ch. 174, folio 2. See also J. Edkins, *Banking and Prices in China*, pp. 128-129, in which two of the dates were incorrectly given as the twentieth day of the seventh month and the twentieth day of the eighth month, while, according to the authentic historical record, they were the thirtieth day of the seventh month and the fifth day of the eighth month respectively.

[2] *History of Sung*, ch. 173, folios, 1-11.

of the two systems instituted by the T'ang dynasty. Although the public land system of the earlier part of the T'ang dynasty was not restored, the poll and land taxes which were levied in the northern provinces of the empire by the Yüan emperors were said to be modeled after the triple tax system of the early T'ang period. In the South the semi-annual and tax system of the later T'ang period was employed. The peculiar feature of the northern system was that either a land tax or a poll tax was levied on a family, depending on whether it was rich in numbers or in land. If the number of its adults was large and its acreage was small, a poll tax was levied; if the number of its adults was small but its landed property considerable in amount, a land tax was collected. In addition to the poll and land taxes, a personal-service tax was levied throughout the empire. This tax was imposed in proportion to the amount of property owned by each family and was required to be paid in silk or silver.[1] Since the family was the basis on which these three taxes were levied, the tax system of the Yüan dynasty may be designated as a composite of family taxes. Although the land tax was levied at a rather moderate rate, the personal-service tax was an exceedingly exorbitant one. It may be said, therefore, that the tax system of the Yüan dynasty was neither systematic nor uniform when compared with any one of the tax systems of the T'ang period, and that it was not until the reign of the founder of the Ming dynasty that a thorough reform of land and personal-service taxes was made.

System of Land and Personal-Service Taxes laid down by the Founder of the Ming Dynasty.—What were considered the most thorough and elaborate fiscal regulations put into effect after the T'ang dynasty were those instituted by

[1] *History of Yüan*, ch. 93, folios 2-3.

the founder of the Ming dynasty. This ruler introduced two kinds of tax records. One, which was known as the personal-service tax register, listed the families of the state under three headings: (1) those in residence at the time of the last census; (2) those new in the area, and (3) those that had removed since the last census. It also recorded the number of families in the area, a figure obtained by deducting the number of families that had removed from the total of the families newly arrived and those already on record. This register furnished the data necessary for levying a personal-service tax on each family. The other record, which was called the land register, classified the landed property of each family as to quality and listed all sales or mortgages of holdings. On the basis of this register land taxes were imposed and rival claims on landed property were settled.[1]

In putting his tax program into operation this brilliant monarch made a great mistake, which has remained uncorrected even up to the present time. Because it was only after a fierce struggle that he had been able to subdue the people of the Hangchow, Chia-hsing, and Hu-chow prefectures in the province of Chekiang, and those of Soochow and Sung-kiang in the province of Kiang-su, he harbored a deep resentment against these localities. He therefore punished them by confiscating the private property of some of the wealthy citizens and by taxing the holdings of the small land-owners at a rate five, or in some cases ten, times as great as that imposed in other parts of the country.

As the land tax of these prefectures was based on the rent charged by the private landlords, the excessive rates exacted absorbed all the rental income of the small owners. The second Ming emperor lightened the burden of the oppressed areas in 1399 A. D.; but when the third emperor came to the throne four years later, the high rates were

----

[1] *History of Ming*, ch. 78, folio 1.

restored on the ground that the land of these regions was of better quality than that of other parts of the empire. This superiority was, and still is, a fact; but the taxes then imposed were out of all proportion to the value of the land and were only partially counterbalanced by subsequent land improvements. Later attempts at the reduction of the land tax in these prefectures have been unsuccessful; and at present a new factor has come into play, namely, that the majority in the provincial legislature determines the tax policies. As the representatives from the prefectures of Soochow and Sung-kiang, and those from Hangchow, Chia-Hsing, and Hu-chow constitute only a minority in the provincial legislatures of Kiang-su and Chekiang respectively, it is scarcely to be expected that the representatives from other prefectures of the province will agree to the reduction of the land tax rate in these special regions, for such reduction would eventually result in the increase of rates in the other districts. The plight of the overtaxed prefectures shows how a fiscal practice having its origin in an early injustice may remain uncorrected for a number of centuries.[1]

Evasion of Land Taxes during the Ming Dynasty. — In the year 1393 the acreage of cultivated land recorded in the land register was 8,507,623,068 *mou*; one hundred and forty years later, only 4,228,058,000 *mou* were listed, showing a decrease of nearly one-half. This falling-off was attributed by the historians to three causes: first, the greater part of the land acquired by the aristocrats was not registered and was therefore virtually exempt from taxation; second, the people made dishonest reports of their property to the government; and, third, the prevalence of banditry in some parts of the country prevented farming and thus decreased the amount of land cultivated. It was not until the

[1] *Continuation of the General Research,* ch. ii, folio 12.

year 1580, during the reign of Emperor Shêng Tsung, that the cultivated acreage was increased to 7,000,000,000 *mou,* or roughly 82.3 per cent of that recorded in 1393. This improvement was entirely due to the statesmanship of Chang Chu-Chêng, then prime minister.[1]

The Reform of the Salt Tax Administration during the Five Dynasties, and the Sung, Yüan and Ming Dynasties.— During the period from the middle of the T'ang dynasty to the beginning of the Ming dynasty, several important changes were made in the administration of the salt tax. After the breaking down of the salt-tax system of Liu An, the revenue derived from this lucrative source was monopolized by the local military leaders. During the years between the fall of the T'ang empire and the rise of the Sung Empire, when the Five Dynasties were following one another in rapid succession, two other systems of salt taxation were introduced. One was the per-capita tax system of the Posterior Chou dynasty, in accordance with which the families of the state were divided into five classes on a basis of their probable annual consumption of salt, and each family paid yearly the salt tax required of its class. Families of the first class paid 1,000 cash a year; those of the second, third, fourth and fifth classes paid 800, 600, 400 and 200 cash respectively. Payment was made at stated intervals throughout the year. The second method of salt taxation was the semi-annual levy of the Posterior Chou dynasty. According to this the salt and the land taxes were combined into one and were paid twice a year, in the summer and in the autumn.[2]

In the early part of the Sung dynasty, both the monopolistic and *laissez faire* policies were followed in regard to the salt industry. The former prevailed in the northern

---

[1] *Continuation of the General Research,* ch. ii, folio 2.

[2] *General Research,* ch. xv, folio 150; ch. xvi, folios 53-54.

part of the empire, and the latter in most districts of the south. The coexistence of these systems resulted in the failure of both, and consequently a third policy was introduced in the year of 1048 A. D. The chief provisions of this were, first, that a special bureau for the administration of a salt tax should be created by the central government at the capital; second, that certificates representing 200 catties of salt each should be issued by the bureau for sale to the merchants; third, that the holders of these certificates should be entitled to draw salt from the salt-producing localities and sell it at any place they saw fit; and, fourth, that the price of salt should be so regulated that as soon as it fell below the point of thirty-five cash a catty in the market of the capital, the issue of salt certificates should be suspended, and as soon as it rose above the margin of forty cash a catty, the selling of these certificates should be encouraged. The latter provision was intended to guard against the issue of certificates in excess of the demand of the market, to prevent exorbitant profits, to keep the price of salt at a normal level, and to protect the mass of the people from the profiteering of the salt merchants. The salt certificates were modeled on the paper money then in existence and might be properly called bills of salt exchange. Fan Siang, the originator of this policy and a successful administrator of the salt tax of the time, set the admirable precedent of maintaining a reserve of 2,000,000 catties of salt for every 6,000 certificates issued. But this system was not followed in later periods. In the years 1077 and 1080 A. D., more than 1,770,000 certificates were issued, while the salt produced was barely sufficient to meet the requirement of 1,175,000 certificates, thus leaving 590,000 certificates for which there was no revenue. Through inflation of this kind the value of the salt certificates depreciated rapidly, especially in the last part of the Sung dynasty.[1] In this connection, it should

[1] *History of Sung*, ch. 181, folios 4-8; ch. 182, and ch. 183, folios 1-4.

be pointed out, however, that with some alterations, usually vexatious both to the salt merchants and to the people at large, the practice of issuing salt certificates survives even up to the present.[1]

After the Sung dynasty lost the northern part of China to the Golden Tartars, in 1126, the government relied for its revenue chiefly on the salt tax; and increases in the rate of this tax were frequent during the dynasty. But when compared with the rates put into effect by the succeeding Yüan dynasty, those exacted during the Sung dynasty became insignificant. According to the *History of Yüan,* the Emperor Ogdai in the year 1230 A. D. levied a tax of 10 taels of silver on the salt merchant for each certificate representing four hundred catties of salt, which commodity was then monopolized by the government. In 1261, the Emperor Kublai reduced the tax to 7 taels of silver. After conquering the southern part of the Sung empire, and thus augmenting his supply of salt, he fixed the price of a certificate at 9,000 cash in Chung-t'ung paper currency, or four and one-half taels of silver, a material reduction. But demands on the government treasury continued pressing, and the easiest means of securing increased revenue was either to issue more and more paper money or to raise the price of a salt certificate. Both policies were adopted; and the latter was put into effect in the year 1289, by an imperial order, which increased the price of the certificates to 50,000 cash each. In 1296 this price was raised to 65,000 cash. During the seven years from 1309 to 1315 successive increases in the price of a certificate were made by imperial edicts, until it reached 150,000 cash. That is to say, the market value of a certificate during the twenty years from 1296 to 1315 increased from 65,000 to 150,000 copper coins. This was the result of two suicidal fiscal policies: the inflation

[1] Chia, S. Y., *Fiscal History of the Chinese Republic,* bk. ii, pp. 270-271.

of paper money on the one hand, and the excessive issue of salt certificates on the other.

The Sung dynasty enacted several laws governing the salt industry. During the Yüan dynasty these laws were made more rigid, and severe punishments were imposed upon the transgressors. The privilege of selling salt had territorial limits. The prefectures and districts where it could be sold were fixed by law. Any one who was found trafficking in salt outside these areas forfeited half of his salt to the government and the remaining half to the person reporting his offense. For the salt smuggler the punishment was exile for two years and seventy " stripes " as corporal punishment. In addition, half his property was confiscated, and of this, half was given to the informer. Capital punishment was inflicted upon persons printing or circulating false certificates, and the whole amount of the criminal's property was given to the informer as a reward.[1] All these cruel enactments proved futile when the people at large finally rose in arms against the greedy and rapacious government. Thus indirect taxation, a burden under which the poor are helpless in ordinary times, may constitute the spark that will set a whole empire afire and bring about its final downfall.

Fiscal Evolution and Retrogression during the Latter Part of the Ming Dynasty and Throughout the Ts'ing Régime (1580 A. D.–1912 A. D.)

During the period from the middle of the Ming dynasty to the end of the Ts'ing Empire several fiscal changes occurred which deserve our attention. These were (1) the reform of land and personal-service taxes in the years 1580-1725; (2) the exaction of exorbitant mining taxes during the latter part of the Ming dynasty; (3) the reform of

[1] *History of Yüan*, ch. 94, folios 3-5; ch. 97, folios 2-7.

fiscal administration during the early part of the Ts'ing dynasty; (4) the sale of titles and offices and the adoption of other undesirable fiscal measures; (5) the imposition of *likin* or internal transit duties following the T'ai-p'ing revolution; (6) the gradual loss of tariff autonomy after the Opium War; (7) the growth of the public debt owing to the Boxer uprising and the Sino-Japanese War; (8) the domestic loan experiments of 1894 and 1898, and the beginning of the provincial loans; (9) the growth of the industrial loans and their relations to the so-called " Scramble for Concessions "; and (10) the fiscal reforms attempted during the latter part of the Ts'ing dynasty and their bearing upon the fiscal problems of the present Republic.

The Reform of Land and Personal-Service Taxes during the Latter Part of the Ming Dynasty and the Beginning of the Ts'ing Dynasty.—A tax program known as the " single whip system " was instituted by Chang Chu-chêng in 1580, during the reign of the emperor Shên Tsung of the Ming dynasty. Following the example of Yang Yen of the T'ang period, he set a money equivalent for the personal-service tax of each district and divided this sum equitably among the land-holders according to the quality and amount (or acreage) of their land. When there arose a demand for public labor, the government employed paid workmen and the people were freed from the burden of corvées. The exaction of various commodities in the name of contributions, tribute in kind, etc., was abolished, and such supplies as were required for official purposes were purchased out of the revenue from the land tax. Thus land was made the only basis of direct taxation, and the land tax became a composite of the land and personal-service taxes. This reform was maintained for a short period only; but it marked the beginning of the third stage of the development of the Chinese land tax system for the reason that the amalgamation of the so-called "adult tax," i. e., a composite of the poll and the personal-service taxes, with the land tax, as effected in the early part of the Ts'ing dynasty, was as a matter of fact merely a continuation of the reform started by Emperor Shên Tsung of the Ming dynasty.

The "single whip system" of the Ming dynasty was broken down by the repeated increases in the land tax. Because of a rebellion in Manchuria, Emperor Shên Tsung raised the tax rate of the Empire three times between 1618 and 1620. In an ineffectual effort to stem the Manchu invasion Emperor Chuang-lieh increased it four times between 1630 and 1639. In the last-named year the total military expenditure amounted to 20,000,000 taels of silver, which was considered an unprecedented single item of outlay at that time; and indeed the relative enormity of this sum is apparent when we take into consideration the fact that in the early part of the Ming dynasty the total amount of the national expenditure never exceeded 2,000,000 taels. The overthrow of the Ming Empire by the Manchus serves to show that the financing of a war solely through increasing the direct tax is apt to arouse the dissatisfaction of the people at large and to weaken the national unity against foreign invasion.

Seeing that the last emperors of the Ming dynasty lost the support of their people by their excessive increase of land taxation, the founder of the Ts'ing or Manchu dynasty did away with all the additional taxes on land in 1644, and set the amount of the land tax according to the land-tax register of the Ming dynasty as contained in the fiscal record compiled in the year 1581.[1]

In 1646 the national laws relating to land taxation were codified, and a personal-service tax was declared, to be levied on the adult population as enumerated in the national census

---

[1] *Political Institutes of the Ts'ing Dynasty*, ch. iv, folio 12.

taken once every five years. In 1712 the second emperor of the Ts'ing dynasty pledged that the amount of the adult tax should be fixed as of the year 1711 and that no poll tax should be imposed on persons born thereafter. In 1725, by a decree of the third emperor of the Ts'ing dynasty, the adult tax or, as it has sometimes been called, the poll tax, in the different provinces was merged with the land tax, and this combined tax was henceforth called the " land-poll tax." The method of apportioning the adult tax varied in the different provinces. In the province of Chihli, which we may take as an example, there was added to each tael of silver levied for the payment of land tax, .27 of a tael for the adult tax, making a total of 1.27 taels for every tael of land tax. In some provinces a certain procedure was provided for the transitional period. Thus the " single whip system " of the Ming dynasty succeeded in combining the personal-service tax and the land tax into a composite land tax, and the tax reform of the Ts'ing dynasty accomplished a further amalgamation by incorporating the adult or poll tax in the composite land tax of the preceding dynasty.

Unlawful Exaction of Mining Taxes during the Latter Part of the Ming Dynasty. — Beside making excessive increases in land taxes, the later Ming emperors levied exorbitant taxes on the gold, silver, copper, iron and tin mines. The heaviest imposts were those laid on the gold and silver mines. During the early part of the Ming dynasty the working of silver mines was not favored by the government on the ground that the operators of these mines were usually exposed to the risk of losing all or a part of their invested capital, while the government obtained very little revenue from this source. In 1596, when the condition of the government finances had become precarious and the need of new sources of revenue was urgent, the operating of silver and gold mines was given special encouragement by Emperor

Shên Tsung. Unfortunately, the means employed to this end were disastrous: they destroyed rather than developed the industry. The government appointed a number of eunuchs as superintendents of the silver and gold mines in the various provinces and required the wealthy families to be responsible for the working of the mines. At first the government exacted a mining tax of 40 per cent on the yield of the mines and allowed the mining operators the rest of the profit. But this did not satisfy the demands of the grasping eunuchs, and the next move was to compel the rich families to buy up the government's share of the output of the mines in the form of raw materials, rather than as refined metals. When these families became bankrupt one after the other, the whole district was required to pay the tax assigned to it by the eunuch superintendent of the mines, no matter whether the mines within its boundary were in operation or not, or whether their output was sufficient to justify the imposition of that amount of taxation. Some families were punished for alleged operation of the mines without, or beyond, the government permit, by the confiscation of their properties without the due process of law or sufficient evidence of facts. Some other holders of land which was supposed to have mineral resources were required to pay an annual mining tax regardless of whether such lands were producing minerals or not. In short, the rich families of the time were the prey of the eunuch superintendents and the hundreds and thousands of rapacious tax-gatherers in their service.[1] These evil practices were largely responsible for the overthrow of the Ming dynasty. And more than this, they deterred the Chinese people from engaging in mining for several centuries. Only within recent decades has this industry been revived.

Reform of Fiscal Administration during the Early Part

[1] *History of Ming*, ch. 81, folios 3-4.

of the Ts'ing Dynasty.—In the year 1650, the government revenue amounted to 14,859,000 taels of silver; expenditures totaled 15,734,000 taels, of which 13,000,000 taels was spent for military purposes, and 2,000,000 taels for administrative purposes; the deficit was 815,000 taels. Fiscal conditions were still far from satisfactory; but the small amount of the administrative expenditure showed rigid economy on the part of the government, while the huge military expenditure constituted a common and necessary feature of the building up of a great empire.

The second emperor also followed a policy of careful economy. He tentatively limited the imperial outlay to one-tenth of that of the Ming dynasty, which had amounted to 1,000,000 taels. But this economy program was rather too extreme. He abolished the compilation and publication of the annual abstract of the fiscal reports of the various provinces and also the publication of the decennial census, although it was required that the annual reports still be sent to the central government, and that the population census in the form of an estimate be taken every five years in place of the old decennial census. Since this ruler regarded the making of an abstract of the annual fiscal reports of the different provinces as useless, the fiscal officers no longer considered the reports of serious importance. This relaxation of fiscal administration made it possible for those in charge of public funds to transfer public money into their private accounts without detection.

It was not until the year 1723, i. e., the first year of the rule of the third emperor, that an office for the auditing of public accounts was established for the first time in the Ts'ing dynasty. Five hundred and fifty miscellaneous fiscal reports made by the provinces to the central government were examined; ninety-six of these, which were found to be unsatisfactory, were rejected, and the officials submitting them were ordered to make good all the deficits found in them. It was discovered that during the period from 1717 to 1726 the fiscal officers of the Kiang-su province alone embezzled as large a sum as 4,700,000 taels of silver. Unfortunately, in the year 1726 the emperor, relying too much upon his policy of strict and heavy punishment of corrupt officials, ordered the auditing office abolished with a warning that officers who violated administrative regulations would incur the severe penalties prescribed by law whenever their offenses were discovered by their supervising officers. Although throughout the remaining part of his reign the integrity of the fiscal administrators was well maintained even without the system of auditing, the later degradation of the fiscal administration may well be traced to his shortsightedness and disregard of the necessity of judicial control over public accounts even where there was effective administrative supervision.

Sale of Titles and Offices and the Adoption of Other Undesirable Fiscal Measures.—Several pernicious practices gained foothold during the early years of the Ts'ing dynasty. These we will summarize briefly: (1) *The sale of titles and offices.*—The practice of selling titles dated back to the year 166 B. C., when Emperor Wên of the former Han dynasty, upon the recommendation of Chao Tso,[1] decreed that the

[1] Dr. Chen Huan-chang considered that this policy of Chao Tso was drawn from the Confucian doctrines. But as a matter of fact, Confucius warned against the bestowal of titles on those who did not deserve them and against placing expediency before principle; it seems improbable, therefore, that he would sanction such a course as Chao Tso advocated. Dr. Chen committed a similar error in classifying Sang Hung-yang, the advocate of salt and iron monopoly policies during the Han period, as a Confucian, not recognizing that these were policies that the Confucians condemned as most detrimental to the welfare of the people at large. Chao Tso was listed in the History of Han as a Jurist; while Sang Hung-yan, though a Jurist administrator, was not listed in the school of Jurists nor in any other school by Pan Ku in the History of Han, and was not a political scholar of the Confucian faith at all. See Chen, H. C., *op. cit.,* pp. 360 and 557; also Pan Ku, *History of Han,* ch. xxx, folio 8.

people who sent their grain to the reserve granaries in the
districts along the northern boundary of the empire, where
the invasion of the Huns was imminent, should be rewarded
with honorary official titles, the rank of which should be determined in accordance with the amount of grain which they
contributed in order to meet the need of the government.
This was followed during the reigns of his successors [1] by
the policy of requiring a certain amount of grain for the
commutation of prison sentences.   Then followed a still
worse policy, put into effect by the unworthy Emperor Lin
of the Latter Han dynasty in 178 A. D., namely, the sale of
public offices at definite prices with definite discounts.[2]   In
later dynasties, this practice was repeatedly resorted to by
unprincipled emperors or ministers.   In the reign of the
fourth emperor of the Ts'ing dynasty, it became an important means of revenue.   At first the policy was adopted for
such purposes as providing funds for famine relief, prevention of floods along the Yellow River, military expeditions,
or reserve for public granaries.   But as time went on, income from this source was turned to other uses; and worst
of all, those who got their appointments through the payment of large sums of money were more or less obliged to
make their " official investments " pay by exacting illegal or
semi-illegal contributions from the people who happened to
be placed under their jurisdiction.   This practice of office-
selling during the Ts'ing dynasty resulted in the demoraliza-
tion of the administrative force of the Manchu government
in its later periods, and is indirectly and partially responsible for the difficulties involved in the purification of popular elections under the present Republic.   (2) *Contributions
exacted from the salt merchants, large importers, and other*

[1] *History of Han,* ch. xxiv, pt. i, folio 3.

[2] *History of Latter Han,* ch. viii, folio 2.

business entrepreneurs. — These contributions constituted merely another form of the sale of titles or offices. In some cases the merchants made their contributions of their own volition; but in most cases they were asked to make them, and in return they were given titles and guarantee of promotion in the civil service at the earliest possible time. These practices made it impossible to maintain effectively and fully the systems of civil-service examinations and official promotion according to merit, the introduction of which dated back to the reign of Emperor Yao in the twenty-third century B. C.[1] (3) *The extra charges on import duties.*— In 1702 the amount of the extra charges on import duties was 400,000 taels; it was increased to 1,170,000 taels in 1720. (4) *The increase of the rate of salt tax.*—The price to the merchants of each catty of salt was increased at first half a cash; then often one cash was added, and in some instances two or more were added. These increased prices were in the beginning considered as temporary; but they soon gained foothold, and only recently have the fiscal scientists come to question the justice of these rates. (5) *The indirect increase of the rate of land tax.*—Although the land-tax rate remained unaltered throughout the Ts'ing dynasty, in accordance with the promise of the second emperor, the rights of the people were by no means safeguarded thereby; for the fiscal officers of the time were able by a variety of subterfuges to effect a virtual increase in the land tax without violating the emperor's sacred promise. These devices were as follows: (a) the exaction of extra charges for melting the local taels into the standard silver tael, the pure-silver content of which was fixed by the government. As the silver currency was not uniform throughout the country, an extra charge for converting the one into the other was not

[1] *Chinese Classics*, vol. iii, pt. i, bks. i and ii.

unjustifiable. But the fiscal officers charged more than was necessary. This practice was introduced in the latter part of the Ming dynasty and was therefore denounced by the founder of the Ts'ing line in his decree of the year of 1644 as a form of extortion. In 1665 the people were permitted by law to lodge a complaint in court if any excessive charges were made by the fiscal officers. In 1678 another decree was issued holding liable the provincial high officials for the concealment of any guilt on the part of their subordinates in levying the so-called "melting loss." But all these decrees proved futile because no salaries were provided for the fiscal officers of various ranks who, as a consequence, depended on the additional charge for their personal incomes. The difficulty of the situation was recognized by the second emperor of the Ts'ing dynasty. But it was not until the reign of the third emperor that this extra charge to counterbalance the loss of silver from melting was legalized as a compensation tax to be employed for official salaries or other public purposes. This legalization of an extra charge into a regular charge on land tax was welcome at the time because it had the effect of setting a limit upon an exaction which was formerly made at the will of the fiscal officers of various ranks without any restraint. (b) Extra charge for the inadequate weight of local taels. This was simply a method of demanding an increase in the extra charge for compensating for the loss of silver in melting; but it was not so designated merely to avoid the contention of the public that in practice melting did not necessarily take place. The charge was first imposed in the province of Szechuan, where 6 ounces of silver were exacted for every hundred taels of silver paid as land tax. It was legalized in 1738 as another compensation tax or a legitimate additional charge on land tax, and took its place as an item of public revenue instead of going into the private pockets of the tax-gatherer as it had in former times. This also was regarded as a fiscal reform at that time, and was therefore adopted in all other provinces. (c) The extra charge for the loss of grain in handling, storing, or shipping. As the land tax was paid in kind in certain parts of the country, an extra charge was made for the possible loss in the handling, shipping, or the storage of grain. In some cases, if the tax was paid in money instead of in kind, another extra charge was made, in practice if not in name, by exacting of the tax-payer a greater money equivalent for the grain than it would bring in the market. This was considered a lucrative source of revenue for the tax-collectors throughout the Ts'ing dynasty, and was not abolished until the early part of the Republican period. Thus it will be seen that the exaction of a tax in kind or in silver bullion or in anything other than a uniform and stable currency is exposed to the abuse of tax-gatherers of all ranks, high and low.

Adam Smith, the father of economic science, pointed out the evils of the practice of collecting taxes in kind. He said:

. . . A public revenue which was paid in kind would suffer so much from the mismanagement of the collectors, that a very small part of what was levied upon the people would ever arrive at the treasury of the prince. Some part of the public revenue of China, however, is said to be paid in this manner. The Mandarins and other tax gatherers will, no doubt, find their advantage in continuing the practice of a payment which is so much more liable to abuse than any payment in money.[1]

(d) Additional charges for specific purposes.—In the latter part of the Ts'ing dynasty the need of modernizing the educational, industrial, judicial and police systems in the im-

---

[1] Smith, A., *Wealth of Nations*, bk. v, ch. ii, Cannan's edition, vol. ii, p. 323.

perial domain and in the provinces was pressing, while the pledge of making no further increase in the rate of land tax could not be broken without arousing the opposition of the people at large. The only way out of the difficulty was for the government to raise a specific revenue for these specific administrative needs of newer origin and to collect that revenue together with, and in proportion to, the land tax at such rates as would satisfy the increasing administrative demands without causing dissatisfaction among the mass of the people.

These undesirable tax measures so evil in their effects upon the general, as well as the fiscal, administration, exemplify the impracticability of attempting to meet dynamic administrative demands with a fiscal institution of an absolutely static nature. They demonstrated that the policy of non-increase in land tax could not be indefinitely maintained; and that stability of revenue could hardly counterbalance the disadvantage of inelasticity. They illustrated the danger of the *quid pro quo* principle as employed in the sale of official titles and other similar practices. And they showed that publicity for every cent of public revenue is indispensable to a satisfactory fiscal system, for it was only with the limiting and legalizing of the " extra charge " exactions under the third emperor of the Ts'ing dynasty that the appalling injustices practiced in the name of these exactions were done away with.

The Introduction of Likin or Internal Transit Duties.—As a result of the defeat which China suffered from her clash with Great Britain in the so-called Opium War, the Treaty of Nanking was signed in 1842. Nearly eight years later, in 1850, the bloody T'ai-p'ing revolution or anti-Manchu movement broke out. During this period of external and internal warfare the Manchu government was confronted with a fiscal crisis: the collection of land taxes in the revolting provinces was impossible, while the increase of the rate of that tax in the other provinces was impracticable because such a measure would turn the people of those areas to the side of the revolutionists and thus hasten the downfall of the government. In order to avoid this peril and yet finance the military force necessary for putting down the formidable internal revolution, the Manchu government was driven to introduce a form of indirect taxation which was strongly attacked by the Confucian scholars and which from the very outset was recognized by the government as an inadvisable measure, namely, the *likin* or " *li* contribution ", which literally means a contribution of one-thousandth of one tael of silver. In view of the method of its collection, it should be called an internal transit duty on commodities.

Likin was first instituted in 1853 at a port in the prefecture of Yang Chow in Kiang-su Province and was soon adopted by other provinces as well. Owing to the fact that it was levied at the low rate of one per cent, that the offices for its collection were established at the important commercial ports only, and that it was administered by persons chosen from the gentry class, which commanded the confidence of society, it did not become a heavy burden upon the people at that time; and the success of the Manchu government in reuniting the nation was largely due to this fiscal measure.

When the *likin* was first introduced as an emergency measure for financing the war, the Manchu government promised that it should be abolished as soon as the revolution was over. But when the rebellion was finally put down, the government failed to fulfil its promise. On the contrary, it raised the rate of the *likin* steadily and established offices for its collection even at the less important commercial ports. This increase of " *likin* ports " made it necessary for goods in transit to undergo a great number of inspections and thus to a large extent impaired the free movement of commodities.

Furthermore, the tax-collectors were usually corrupt and incompetent, and as a rule demanded illegal charges for immediate inspection. Merchants who were unwilling to pay these extra charges had their cargoes held up at the port. As a consequence, the merchants were driven to underdeclare the value of their goods, so that by paying less than their legitimate tax they might have the wherewithal to bribe the officials. It was estimated that, during the last part of the Ts'ing dynasty, for every four taels of silver legally collected, additional charges amounting to 6.50 taels were imposed; that is to say, in collecting the *likin*, an undesirable tax in itself, an extra assessment of 162 per cent was exacted through the maladministration of the tax.[1]

Unquestionably this system of internal taxation constituted one of the most important causes of China's economic decadence, and, the government's failure to abolish the tax which became increasingly exorbitant during the last part of the Manchu régime, resulted in a growing antagonism against the dynasty. Thus we may say, that although the house of Manchu saved itself from extinction in the T'aip'ing revolution by imposing the *likin*, it was doomed to fall upon its failure to abolish a tax which it had morally bound itself to repeal. At the outbreak of the Revolution of 1911, some of the provincial leaders who rose against the Manchu régime effected the abolition of *likin* in their respective provinces; but unfortunately it was later reinstituted in a modified form.[2]

The Gradual Loss of Tariff Autonomy. — As stated be-

[1] Morse, H. B., *Trade and Administration of China*, 3rd rev. ed., 1920, pp. 123-124.

[2] Chia, S. Y., *op. cit.*, pp. 627-642.

fore, the land customs duties had their origin in the fiscal system of the Chou dynasty.[1] Maritime customs duties, however, were not levied until 971 A. D. In that year the first maritime customs house was established in Canton, then the center of China's foreign trade. In the reign of Jen Tsung (1023-1063) maritime customs houses were set up in Hangchow and Ningpo, the other leading commercial ports in China at that time. The rate of import duty was fixed at 20 per cent in 991. In 1023 the rate was reduced to 10 per cent, and a system of compulsory selling to the government was adopted, whereby the government had the option of buying 30 per cent of the imported commodities at low prices set by itself. In 1164, this system of governmental option on import was abolished and the customs rate was fixed at 10 per cent.

During the Yüan dynasty several new tariff laws were enacted. The most noteworthy of these was the law of 1277, which provided that commodities of high quality should be taxed at one-tenth of their value and those of low quality at one-fifteenth, and that foreign goods should be taxed twice as much as domestic goods. In 1369, in the Ming dynasty, a decree was issued which exempted from duty the goods imported by those who brought to the emperor tributes from foreign nations, but it was required that 60 per cent of these imported goods be sold to the government at reduced prices. When we compare the tariff system of the Ming dynasty with that of the Sung dynasty, we find that the former reduced by 10 per cent the import duty required by the latter, but increased the amount of goods which might be purchased by the government from 30 per cent to 60 per cent of that imported.

On the whole, the Ming emperors maintained a friendly attitude toward foreign merchants, although they adopted a

[1] See *supra* ,pp. 62-63.

policy which limited the number of Japanese trading vessels entering Chinese ports to two in every ten years and the number of persons aboard these vessels to two hundred, all of whom were required to return to their country when the transactions were completed. A number of disturbances along the Chinese coast caused by the Japanese smugglers were due to this too severe restriction, the purpose of which was, of course, to check the development of international trade which was then considered as an unworthy occupation for respectable citizens and was usually looked down upon by the Chinese scholars, for the reason that smugglers who engaged in international trade were often found to be of the same class of people as the pirates.[1]

When we come to study the history of the tariff in the Ts'ing dynasty, a period in which the commercial relations between China and the western countries became increasingly closer, we find that before 1842 the foreign merchants were, to a certain extent, unfavorably discriminated against by the Chinese tariff laws or, more exactly, by the administrators of those laws. The Rev. Charles Gutzlaff pointed out in the early part of the nineteenth century that, although the imperial tariff rate at that time was very reasonable and was required by law to be posted at the customs house and to be communicated to the merchants, the revenue officers, on their own responsibility, more than doubled the imposts, without informing the merchants.[2] After the introduction of the *likin* in 1842 the Chinese merchants were placed on a less favorable footing than the foreign merchants, for the import, export, and transit duties imposed on foreign merchants were limited by treaty stipulations, while no check was placed on the amount of *likin* which might be exacted from the Chinese merchants.

[1] *History of Ming*, ch. 81, folio 6.
[2] Gutzlaff, C., *China Opened*, London, Smith, Elder and Co., 1838, vol. ii, p. 67. See also Chu, C., *Tariff Problem in China*, pp. 21-26.

Let us now consider the outstanding developments in the tariff situation in the latter part of the Ts'ing dynasty.

(a) *The Treaty of Nanking and its Bearing on Chinese Tariff.*—Article X of the Treaty of Nanking, 1842, opened the sad history of Chinese tariff of the past 84 years (1842-1926). It reads:

His Majesty the Emperor of China agrees to establish at all Ports[1] which are by the second Article of this Treaty, to be thrown open for the resort of British merchants, a fair and regular Tariff of Export and Import and other Dues, which Tariff shall be publicly notified and promulgated for general information, and the Emperor further engages that, when British Merchandise shall have paid at any of the said Ports the regulated Customs and Dues, agreeable to the Tariff to be hereafter fixed, such Merchandise may be conveyed by Chinese Merchants to any Province or city in the interior of the Empire of China on paying a further amount as Transit Duties which shall not exceed . . . per cent on the tariff value of such goods.[2]

This Article did not specify the rate to be imposed. In the following year, a special declaration was signed at Hongkong, stating that the rate of customs duties should not exceed the one then prevailing, which was approximately 5 per cent *ad valorem*. The Supplementary Treaty of Oct. 8, 1843, with Great Britain reaffirmed that rate, which thus became the standard rate of tariff on imports as well as exports. In 1844, China made a similar arrangement with the United States in her first treaty with that country.[3] She concluded tariff treaties with like provisions with France in 1844, and with Sweden and Norway in 1847.[5]

[1] Namely, Canton, Amoy, Foochow, Ningpo and Shanghai.
[2] *Hertslet's China Treaties*, vol. i, pp. 7-10.
[3] *Ibid.*, pp. 551-552.
[4] *Ibid.*, pp. 527-528.
[5] *Ibid.*, p. 260.

(b) *The Most-Favored-Nation Clause and the Chinese Tariff.*—Beside consenting to an exceedingly low tariff rate, China made another commitment in Article VIII of the Supplementary Treaty of Oct. 8, 1843, with Great Britain, giving the latter one-sided most-favored-nation privileges. That Article reads:

> The Emperor of China having been graciously pleased to grant to all foreign countries whose subjects or citizens have hitherto traded at Canton, the privilege of resorting for purpose of trade to the other ports of Foochow, Amoy, Ningpo and Shanghai on the same terms as the English, it is further agreed that, should the Emperor hereafter be pleased to grant, from any cause whatever, additional privileges and immunities to any of the subjects or citizens of the foreign countries, the same privileges and immunities will be extended to and enjoyed by the British subjects, but it is to be understood that no demand should, on this plea, be unnecessarily brought forth.[1]

The next treaty following this was the American Treaty of July 3, 1844, in which China accorded her most-favored-nation treatment to the United States on the ground that it was only just and fair to grant to the Americans what had been conceded to the English.[2] The treaty concluded with France in the same year made a similar provision for that country,[3] and thus the bondage of this unilateral most-favored-nation clause was steadily strengthened.[4]

(c) *The Downward Tariff Revision of 1858.* — From 1843 to 1858 the tariff rates remained unmodified. When China lost her second war with Great Britain, in 1858, the

---

[1] *Chinese Imperial Maritime Customs, Treaties and Conventions Between China and the Foreign Nations*, Shanghai, 1908, vol. i, p. 201.

[2] *Ibid.*, vol. i, p. 433, see also *Tung Hua Luk*, vol. 86, 1856, p. 12.

[3] Hertslet, *op. cit.*, vol. i, p. 260.

[4] For a fuller discussion, see Sze, T. Y., *China and the Most-Favored-Nation Clause*, 1925, Fleming H. Revell Company, pp. 41-50.

western powers demanded a revision of the tariff downward. As a consequence, the Treaty of Tientsin, 1858, provided, in Article XXVI, that:

Whereas the Tariff fixed by Article X of the Treaty of Nanking (29th Aug., 1842) and which was estimated so as to impose on Imports and Exports a Duty at about the rate of 5 per cent *ad valorem*, has been found by reason of the fall in value of various articles of merchandise, therein enumerated, to impose a Duty upon those considerably in excess of the rate originally assumed as above to be a fair rate, it is agreed that the said Tariff shall be revised. . . [1]

Admitting that the uniform 5 per cent rate had in the beginning been a *fair* one and that the downward revision was necessary in this case, there is no justification for the repeated refusals of the foreign powers involved in China's tariff treaties to allow an upward revision when the prices of imports rose and China saw fit to make such a revision.

(d) *Provisions for the Decennial Revision of Tariff.*— The Treaty of Tientsin also contained the following stipulation:

Article XXVII. It is agreed that either of the High Contracting Parties to this Treaty may demand a further revision of the Tariff, and of the Commercial Articles of this Treaty at the end of ten years, but if no demand be made on either side within six months after the end of the first ten years, then the Tariff shall remain in force for ten years more, reckoned from the end of the preceding ten years; and so it shall be, at the end of each successive ten years.[2]

In spite of this provision for decennial revision of the tariff, the rates remained unchanged for more than forty years

[1] Hertslet, *op. cit.*, vol. i, p. 26.
[2] *Ibid.*, p. 27.

(1858-1902). The rates set in 1858 amounted to approximately 5 per cent *ad valorem* according to the local prices of that time, but prices never remain stationary, and they had risen to such a degree in the forty-year period that the rate was far less than 5 per cent when a revision was made in 1901. China's failure to call for a revision during this period was explained by Dr. Wellington Koo, Chinese delegate to the Washington Conference, before the Committee on Pacific and Far Eastern Questions, as being due to the fact that the needs of the government had been comparatively few, so that the revenues collected, although small, had been adequate to meet the requirements.[1] But a request for revision would have met with little success, for during the years in question the treaty powers were pressing China for reductions in the land frontier rates. In the Commercial Treaty of 1862, she reduced the rate for the Russian trade to two-thirds of the general tariff, i. e., to about 3.3 per cent *ad valorem,* while after her defeat in the Franco-Chinese war in 1885, she granted to the French, in 1885, and to the English, in 1894, special concessions whereby the rate of their land-frontier duty was reduced to .7 and .6 of the prevailing maritime customs rate for their imports and exports respectively.[2] The Statistical Secretary's List of Values, issued by the Chinese Maritime Customs in 1902, shows that the rate of tariff was then so low as 0.06 or 0.04 per cent in some instances, and somewhere between 2 or 3 per cent in many cases.[3] Though the loss of revenue through the neglect of tariff revision was evident, the foreign experts in the Chinese customs service, intentionally or unintentionally, made no recommendation for revision. A

---

[1] Willoughby, W. W., *China at the Conference,* pp. 55-56.

[2] Hsia, C. L., *Studies in Chinese Diplomatic History,* Commercial Press, Shanghai, 1925, p. 198. See also Chu, C., *op. cit.,* pp. 38-40.

[3] See also Chu, C., *op. cit.,* pp. 42-43.

possible explanation of this inaction is that they more or less represented the interests of the foreign powers, who then considered a nominal 5 per cent rate as " fair ", and an effective 5 per cent as a special favor to China. Any idea of increasing the tariff above the 5 per cent rate was regarded as an unimaginable violation of the rights of the foreign powers.

(e) *Regulations for the Rate of Transit Duties.*—Article XXVIII of the Tientsin Treaty placed the rate of transit duties at 2.5 per cent. As these duties involve a tariff problem of China which is yet to be solved, the whole article is here quoted.

Whereas it was agreed in Article X of the treaty of Nanking, that British Imports, having paid the Tariff Duties, should be conveyed into the Interior free of all further charges, except a Transit Duty, the amount whereof was not to exceed a certain percentage on Tariff value; and whereas no accurate information having been furnished of the amount of such Duty, British merchants have constantly complained that charges were suddenly and arbitrarily imposed by the Provincial Authorities as Transit Duties upon produce on its way to the Foreign market, and on Imports on their way into the interior, to the detriment of Trade; it is agreed that within four months from the signing of this Treaty, at all Ports now open to British trade, and within a similar period at all Ports that may hereafter be opened, the authority appointed to superintend the collection of Duties shall be obliged, upon application of the Consul, to declare the amount of Duties leviable on produce between the place of production and the Port of Shipment, and upon Imports between the Consular Port in question and the inland markets named by the Consul; and that a notification thereof shall be published in English and Chinese for general information.

But it shall be at the option of any British Subject, declaring to convey produce purchased inland to a Port, or to convey Imports from a Port to an inland market, to clear his goods of all Transit Duties, by payment of a single charge. The amount of the charge shall be leviable on Exports at the first barrier they may have to pass, or, on Imports, at the Port at which they are landed; and on payment thereof, a certificate shall be issued, which shall exempt the goods from all further inland charges whatsoever.

It is further agreed that the amount of this charge shall be calculated as nearly as possible at the rate of two and a half per cent *ad valorem*, and that it shall be fixed for each article at the conference to be held at Shanghai for the revision of the Tariff.

It is distinctly understood that the payment of Transit Dues, by communication or otherwise, shall in no way affect the Tariff Duties on Imports or Exports, which will continue to be levied separately and in full.[1]

From the above quotation it will be seen that an attempt was made at the solution of the two main problems that are still unsolved today, namely, the limitation of transit duties on imports to a single charge and the limitation of the rate of these duties to one-half of that of customs duties, i. e., to 2.5 per cent *ad valorem*. The first provision did not work out favorably because the provincial authorities sought to raise revenue from time to time by imposing taxes on the goods which were to be consumed in the localities under their jurisdiction, maintaining that these goods, after reaching their destination, should be taxed once more in the form of a computation tax, which directly affected the Chinese people only, which had not been limited by tariff treaties. Through this method of taxation the advantages of the first provision were more or less nullified. This difficulty cannot be done away with unless the power of levying excise taxes is centralized under the control of the national government, which, again, will not be in a position to raise sufficient revenue for meeting the increasing demands of the body

[1] Hertslet, *op. cit.*, vol. i, pp. 27-28.

politic if the present absurd limits on the rates of transit duties and customs duties are to be retained. Therefore, as a matter of practical expediency, the Chinese excise system must be reformed, and the right of tariff autonomy must be restored to China. For the purpose of avoiding administrative friction between the central and provincial governments a proper division should be made between national and local revenue, and the right of levying indirect taxes, excise included, should be vested in the hands of the central government.

(f) *The Declaration of 1898 Relating to the Employment of an Englishman as the Inspector-General of Maritime Customs.*—After 1842, the British government began to interfere in the administration of Chinese maritime customs. But it discontinued this practice in 1851, and the Chinese government collected the customs itself until 1853, when the Tai-ping rebellion became widespread in South China and the customs houses of the treaty ports were forced to close. Owing to the practical necessity, an agreement was made between the Shanghai Taotai or Commissioner and the consuls of Great Britain, the United States and France, whereby the latter were to appoint three representatives from their nationals for the management of the customs at Shanghai. As a result, a board of three foreign inspectors was nominated, but Captain (Sir) Thomas F. Wade, (British), one of the inspectors, took up the main business of organizing the new office. On his resignation one year later, Mr. H. N. Lay, also British, was appointed inspector-general of the customs. The attitude of foreign merchants, especially the Americans, toward this new office is worth noting. The American merchants expressed their opinion in a letter addressed to their minister, Mr. Peter Parker, upon his arrival in 1856. The letter reads in part:

We understood that the new institution was not intended to be permanent. . . . The first and pressing cause for its establishment here (Shanghai) has passed away. . . . Custom-house business in China under Chinese supervision (in other ports) is conducted with a facility which greatly aids in the despatch of business and the ready lading of ships when haste is of importance, while with the minute and in some respects vexatious regulations established by the inspectors, this advantage disappears, and this in itself is no small item in the account against us. . . . [1]

Even the British merchants were not unanimously in favor of retaining the new office. But while some supported the American representation, others voiced their approval of the new system and pressed for its extension to all ports. If the Chinese authorities had been better informed, the customs administration could probably have been placed under Chinese control again when the emergency was over. Unfortunately, this was not the case, and the same system of foreign supervision was established in all other treaty ports then open. This work was carried out by Mr. Lay, who resigned from office in 1863 and was succeeded by Sir Robert Hart.

In 1898 the Chinese government made the declaration that the inspector-general of maritime customs should be a British subject while British trade predominated. In a despatch, dated Feb. 13, 1898, addressed to the British Minister, the government made it clear that " If at some future time the trade of some other country at the various Chinese ports should become greater than that of Great Britain, China will then of course not necessarily be bound to employ an Englishman as inspector-general." [2] Therefore, the question will soon arise as to whether the inspectorate should be headed by

[1] Morse, H. B., *Trade and Administration of China*, 1920, p. 388.
[2] McMurray, J. V. A., *Treaties and Agreements With and Concerning China*, 1921, vol. i, pp. 103-104.

a Chinese or by a representative of the nation whose trade exceeds that of Great Britain when British supremacy in Chinese foreign trade is no longer maintained.

(g) *The Boxer Indemnity and the Tariff Revision of 1901.* — At the end of the Boxer uprising, the Protocol of 1901 was signed and indemnities were demanded from the Chinese government by foreign powers. To obtain funds to meet this new obligation provision was made for a tariff revision that would bring the rates up to an *effective* 5 per cent. This protocol was agreed to by the foreign powers, but with a very important condition, which made a marked change in the Chinese tariff system, namely, that specific duties be substituted for *ad valorem* duties. The condition reads:

All duties levied on imports *ad valorem* shall be converted as far as feasible and with least possible delay into specific duties: The average value of merchandise at the time of landing during the three years 1897, 1898 and 1899, that is to say, the market price less the amount of import duty and incidental expenses, shall be taken as the basis for the valuation of such merchandise. . . . [1]

According to the terms of the said protocol, a revision was made and became effective in 1902. This revision, however, was not a thorough one. It applied only to import duties and to what was known as the " duty free list," while the export tariff was left unrevised. Further, the Sino-Japanese Treaty of 1896 had made it impossible to raise the *ad valorem* rate above 5 per cent because that treaty remained effective up to 1906. The net results of this revision were, therefore, that (1) most of the duties were made specific in character while the rest were 5 per cent *ad valorem;* the goods not enumerated in the tariff were to be taxed at the

[1] Hertslet's *China Treaties*, vol. i, pp. 128 and 148.

rate of 5 per cent *ad valorem;* (2) the restrictions of the earlier treaties were still binding, and (3) the export tariff of 1858 remained unchanged.

(h) *The MacKay Treaty and the Likin Problems.*—In Article VIII of the MacKay Treaty of 1902, the Chinese government, recognizing that "the system of levying *likin* and other dues on goods at the place of production, in transit, and at destination, impedes the free circulation of commodities and injures the interests of trade," pledged itself to "discard completely those means of raising revenue with the limitations mentioned in Section 8, which stated that the Chinese government is at liberty to impose a consumption tax on articles of Chinese origin not intended for export, that this tax shall be levied only at places of consumption and not on goods while in transit, and that it shall not be levied within foreign settlements or concessions."

In order to compensate for the loss of revenue following the proposed abolition of the likin system and the abandonment of all other kinds of internal taxation on foreign imports and on exports, the British government, in return, consented to allow a surtax, not exceeding 7.5 per cent *ad valorem,* on both imports and exports. But despite the pledges of both the Chinese and British governments, these proposals were not put into effect and no further attempt at customs reform was made in the Ts'ing dynasty.

The Growth of Public Debts.—With the introduction of the credit system in modern times, the purchase of government bonds by the investing public has been made possible, and government indebtedness has become one of the leading features of modern finance. The fact that China has just entered the stage of credit economy explains the absence of public credit in her fiscal history up to the latter part of the nineteenth century. Several factors contributed to this slow development of a credit system:

(A) Government indebtedness was regarded as a disgrace by the Chinese rulers throughout the monarchical régime. Montesquieu has well pointed out in his *Spirit of Laws* that honor is the prevailing principle in monarchies,[1] and it is not difficult to see, therefore, why almost all of the Chinese emperors shunned a course which they considered as incompatible with their dignity.[2]

(B) The raising of public loans to defray governmental expenses was deemed an unsound fiscal policy, since the principle of regulating expenditure by revenue had been long recognized by most of the Chinese statesmen as a golden rule of public economy. It was further argued that the fiscal stability of a government could not be maintained unless an ample fund was reserved for emergency purposes. It was therefore held that, if the practice of borrowing were repeatedly resorted to, the government would inevitably be led into bankruptcy.

(C) As the Chinese people had for centuries upheld the doctrine of *laissez faire* or non-interference by the governmental authorities in the field of business, they opposed the raising of money by the government for commercial enterprises.

(D) Competitive armament is responsible for the immense growth of public debts in modern times. China, as a unified nation with a pacific attitude, during the greater part of her history supported no large army for aggression on neighboring states. In periods of national expansion, especially during the periods of the Han, T'ang and Yüan dynasties, her fiscal condition was usually so prosperous as to allow the

[1] Montesquieu, *Spirit of Laws*, Nugent's translation, 1873, vol. i, pp. 29-30.

[2] For historical instances of forced loans adopted during the Tsin and T'ang dynasties, see Hu, C., *Chinese Fiscal History*, pp. 165 and 168. But these should be considered as a proof of the lack, rather than the growth, of public credit.

imposition of new taxes or the increase of the rate of old taxes in order to defray military expenses. During times of prosperity and expansion, therefore, military expenditure was financed through taxation and the raising of public loans for the support of a national standing army was unnecessary.

(E) On the other hand, when internal disturbances occurred, the government took strong and unscrupulous measures to exact money from the people without resorting to the practice of borrowing from them. In other words, during such periods, the people were not asked to subscribe voluntarily to government loans, but were forced to contribute as much as the government could exact from them.

(F) Finally, as Professor H. C. Adams has said, the existence of a representative government is one of the prerequisites of the growth of public indebtedness.[1] China had long been under a monarchical form of government, and under such a system the sphere of governmental function was so limited that revenue derived from certain definite sources of public income was expected to be sufficient to meet all expenditures necessary for the maintenance of government. Any expenditure in excess of this revenue was regarded as a first sign of fiscal instability, since such excess usually brought with it a train of fiscal evils, for example, the imposition of extremely high taxes and the collecting of land taxes before they were due.

All these circumstances precluded the development of public credit under the old Chinese monarchical régime. But as soon as constitutionalism found its way into the country, during the last part of the Ts'ing dynasty, the sphere of state action was gradually extended and the demand for public loans to meet the costs of administrative reorganization and other urgent constructive programs presented itself as a matter of course.

[1] Adams, H. C., *Public Debts*, pp. 7-9.

Unfortunately, the history of the Chinese public debt did not begin with loans for constructive purposes. On the contrary, it began with the borrowing of funds from foreign banks to pay war indemnities and suppress internal disturbances. The growth of foreign loans during the Ts'ing dynasty may be divided into three periods: (1) 1865-1894; (2) 1895-1900; and (3) 1901-1911. The loans raised in the first period were used for the settlement of indemnities demanded by the Russians as compensation for their losses in Ili; for the financing of the Formosan and the Southwest expeditions; and for the execution of China's first naval building program.[1] All these loans were paid off before 1903.[2] The greater part of the proceeds from the loans of the second period were paid to Japan to settle the indemnity which that country exacted from China following the Sino-Japanese War.[3] The loans of the third period were mostly expended for the annual payments of the Boxer indemnity of 450,000,000 Haikwan taels, which, according to the terms of the protocol of 1901, China was forced to pay to the Powers in thirty-nine years, ending in 1940.[4]

The Domestic Loan Experiments of 1894 and 1898, and the Beginning of Provincial Loans.—The first domestic loan, launched in 1894 by the central government, opened the history of the Chinese domestic public debt. The loan was known as the " Merchant Loan of 1894 " and was raised from different provinces to finance the war against Japan. It amounted to only 11,020,000 taels, of which 5,000,000 taels was subscribed by Cantonese merchants and the balance by those of other provinces.[5]

[1] Huang, F. H., *Public Debts in China*, pp. 45-46.
[2] Chia, S. Y., *op. cit.*, pp. 1069-1070.
[3] Huang, F. H., *op. cit.*, pp. 20-21.
[4] Hertslet, *op. cit.*, vol. i, pp. 139-140.
[5] Chia, S. Y., *op. cit.*, bk. iv, pp. 3-4.

Because of the failure of the domestic loan in 1894, the Chinese government was compelled to borrow from foreign banks operating in China to meet the payment of the first, second, and third instalments of the indemnity owed to Japan. When the fourth instalment of this indemnity came due, China again negotiated for a loan with foreign banking groups, but owing to the unreasonable terms demanded by the banks, no agreement was reached. Then the Chinese government turned again to the Chinese merchants and asked them to subscribe to a loan, amounting to 100,000,000 *Kuping* taels, known as the " Trust Loan of 1898." As a special inducement, an official title was conferred upon everyone subscribing 10,000 taels or more. The amount raised by this means was insufficient, showing that the Chinese people had no confidence in the government. As a consequence, the Manchu government made no further attempt to raise money by floating a domestic loan, and became absolutely dependent upon foreign banks as the only source from which it could borrow.

When we consider the indebtedness of the provincial governments, we shall presently see that both domestic and foreign loans had been floated by them since 1905 for such purposes as the reforming of " provincial armies," the replenishing of the empty provincial treasuries and the financing of constructive programs relating to police reorganization and educational and industrial development. It should be noted in this connection, however, that since these foreign loans involved international politics, they could be contracted only with the consent of the central government.

During the Ts'ing dynasty no municipal indebtedness was incurred. The explanation of this is that the municipalities were regarded as subordinate administrative districts whose government affairs were conducted by appointees of the central government, therefore they had no distinct and separate political entities of their own and no right to contract loans for themselves; if they were of commercial importance, the central government would undertake to finance projects for their development through borrowing or by other means, and open them to foreign trade. Those municipalities of less importance, in which the business activities were under the supervision and control of craft and mercantile guilds, were not confronted with problems of modern improvements, and had no need to borrow money.[1]

The Growth of Industrial Loans and their Relations to the So-called " Scramble for Concessions." — In the two years from 1898 to 1899, China granted Germany, Russia, France, Great Britain, and the Italian-Belgian and the American syndicates a number of railway concessions.[2] The struggle of these outside interests for economic domination in China had three outstanding results. The first and most important of these was an awakening of the Chinese people, culminating in the " Reform Movement of 1899," whose program demanded a constitutional form of government as the only means of saving China from being dismembered by the foreign powers. The second was the growth of anti-foreign sentiment eventually manifesting itself in the Boxer uprising of 1900. The third was the declaration of the " Open Door Policy" with regard to Manchuria and other spheres of influence in China by the United States in 1899.

The scramble for concessions ceased for a few years following the Boxer uprising. But shortly after the close of the Russo-Japanese War in 1905, the Powers again began to vie with one another for special interests. As a consequence, a number of new concessions were granted by the Manchu government, and numerous large foreign loans were raised supposedly for the development of industries. The policy

[1] Huang, H. L., *op. cit.*, p. 13.
[2] Hsu, M. C., *Railway Problems in China*, 1915, pp. 34-45.

of rewarding on a common basis officials who negotiated these loans demoralized the personnel of the fiscal administration. The pledging away of China's right of railway construction on a wholesale scale aroused strong opposition among the people. When, on May 10, 1911, the final agreement for the construction of the Hankow-Szechuan and the Hankow-Canton railways was signed by the Chinese government with the Four-Power Banking Group, including French, British, German, and American interests, the gentries of the various provinces concerned protested vehemently, preparing the way for the nation-wide revolution which broke out on the 10th of October of the same year.

The Fiscal Reforms Attempted during the Last Part of the Ts'ing Dynasty and Their Bearing upon the Fiscal Problems of the Present Republic.—In view of the fact that Japan under a constitutional government defeated Russia under the despotic czar, the Chinese government as well as the Chinese people became deeply convinced that only through constitutionalism could China be saved. As a consequence, a movement for the adoption of a constitutional form of government was started, and a program of preparation, to extend over a nine-year period, was proclaimed in 1907. The fiscal reforms provided in this program were as follows: in the second year of preparation, the provinces were to work out tentative budgets; in the third year, a new system of provincial taxation was to be adopted; in the fourth year, reformed methods of public accounting were to be introduced and a national budgetary system was to be inaugurated; and in the fifth year, a new system of national taxation was to be promulgated.[1]

By the Imperial Edict of January 10, 1909, a Central Commission for the Reorganization of the Fiscal Affairs of the

[1] Brunnert, H., *Present Day Political Organization of China*, 1910, pp. 186-187.

Empire was created and sub-commissions were established in the various provinces.[1] The survey of the fiscal conditions of the country made by this commission was of value, but the lavish expenditures of the various departments of the central government were steadily reducing these conditions from bad to worse.

Other evils of the time were: (a) an increasing foreign control over China's customs administration resulting from the pledging of customs receipts as securities for indemnities and loans, (b) the breaking down of the old contribution system, according to which the rich provinces were required to turn in to the central government their surplus revenues, (c) the lack of a central bank for the custody of public funds and their proper management, and (d) the prevalence of depreciated currency and inflated government notes with a consequent loss to national and provincial treasuries.

Certain remedies for some of these evils were put into effect: (1) The Imperial Bank was established in 1904, and in 1908 it was reorganized and given power to issue notes and to regulate the circulation of new coins and government funds; (2) a loan of £10,000,000 was arranged in 1911 with an international banking group for carrying out a reform of the currency system;[2] and (3) the first national budget was made shortly before the Revolution of 1911. But the inefficiency and extravagance of the national government, the abrogation of its right to tax foreigners or its own subjects who resided in foreign settlements, as stipulated in the treaties with the Powers, the lack of coordination between the central and the provincial governments in fiscal matters, and the restrictions on the tariff autonomy of the country, were left unameliorated.

[1] Brunnert, H., *op. cit.*, pp. 186-187.

[2] This loan was not floated on account of the Chinese Revolution in 1911. For more detailed information, see Wei, W. P., *Currency Problem in China, passim.*

Moreover, when the national budget was promulgated it met with vehement attacks. As pointed out by the Finance Committee of the National Council, its main defects were as follows: First, it did not balance revenue and expenditure; the amount of the expenditures was 50,000,000 *Kuping* taels in excess of the revenue, and this huge deficit was left uncovered. Second, wasteful expenditures were not curtailed, and no specific program for administrative reorganization was introduced. Notwithstanding that a number of new offices were created, the old inefficient offices were retained, so that expenditures were enormously increased through the multiplication of offices having duplicate or parallel functions or no functions at all. Third, and worst of all, was the lack of proper division of functions between the central and the provincial governments with regard to fiscal affairs. The central government depended upon the provinces for its revenue. Those provinces which had annual deficits to face were subsidized by the central government, whereas those provinces with annual surpluses were required to pay a portion of these funds into the national treasury. The latter provinces, however, tried in one way or another to avoid meeting this obligation, showing that there was no cooperation or mutual confidence between the central and the provincial governments. Furthermore, the final decision on the increase or reduction of certain items of government expenditure as specified in the so-called national budget, rested not with the central government as should be the case, but with the provincial authorities. Such fiscal disorders as these could only arouse dissatisfaction among the people and lead the government to its ultimate downfall.[1] Thus the difficult fiscal problems which the Manchu government attempted to solve, but without success, became the problems of the Chinese Republic, and are still awaiting solution.

[1] Hu, C., *op. cit.*, pp. 392-408.

THE REPUBLICAN PERIOD (1912- ——)

The Chinese Republic has passed through four distinct stages of political development, namely: (1) a period of decentralization, (2) a period of centralization, (3) a period of disorganization, and (4) a period of reconstruction. Likewise, her fiscal development may be divided into four stages synchronizing with the four stages of political development. These are the stages of (1) fiscal decentralization (1912-1913), (2) fiscal centralization (1913-1916), (3) fiscal disorganization (1916-1925), and (4) fiscal reconstruction (1926-).

From 1912 to 1913 China was in a state of disorganization, an inevitable result of the Revolution. The central government was helpless because the provincial revolutionary leaders were in favor of a system of political as well as fiscal decentralization, the provincial treasuries were in most cases empty and therefore unable to remit money to the central government, the national credit was in a critical condition, and the domestic banking circle was keeping its funds in tight rein. Consequently, the central government was compelled to raise the money needed for reorganization and reconstruction by means of foreign loans, of which the most important was the " Reorganization Loan of 1913 ".

After assuming the presidency of the Chinese Republic, Yuan Shih-kai, with the proceeds of the " Reorganization Loan " at his disposal, succeeded in carrying out his policy of unifying the country by force. He concentrated the power of fiscal administration in the central government, of which he had absolute control, by adopting the following measures:

(i) The reorganization of the fiscal administration after the model followed in France and Japan. A National Revenue Board was created in 1913 with many branches in the various provinces to take charge of national revenues in the respective provinces.[1]

(ii) The exercise of strict supervision by the central government over the revenues and expenditures of the various provinces.

(iii) The restoration and enforcement of the old practice of compulsory apportioned annual contribution to the central government by those provinces which had fiscal surpluses.

(iv) The specification of the following five sources of revenue as exclusively belonging to the central government: (a) the fees for the inspection of title deeds, (b) the proceeds of the stamp tax, (c) the proceeds of wine and tobacco taxes, (d) the wine and tobacco license fees, and (e) the brokers' license fees.[2]

(v) The establishment of the Bureau of Land Measurement in 1914 for the purpose of making a cadastral survey of the country.[3]

As evidence of the successful promulgation of his fiscal policies, the two domestic loans of 1914 and 1915 were over-subscribed, setting a precedent in the history of Chinese domestic loans. This also showed that he commanded the confidence of the people. But this confidence was soon lost when he launched a monarchist movement for his own selfish ends. With the downfall of his government (1916), the highly centralized fiscal administration which he had set up crumbled.

In 1916 the Republic entered upon its third phase. In

[1] Chia, S. Y., *op. cit.*, pp. 104-106.

[2] Chia, S. Y., *op. cit.*, pp. 45-104.

[3] The plan formulated by the Bureau provided net produce for arable lands and net rent for urban lands as basis for land or real estate taxation. Deductions from the gross produce or contractual rent for certain expenses were allowed in ascertaining net produce or rent. For fuller informations, see Chia, S. Y., *op. cit.*, vol. i, pp. 312-313.

this period the central government was fiscally more helpless than it had been in 1912 owing to the fact that a group of militarists had gained control of the provinces, which they regarded as their own sphere of influence and in which they exercised absolute power. Under such political circumstances the tottering central government found it well-nigh impossible to enforce the system of provincial contributions restored by Yuan Shih-kai.

In 1917, the Manchu Restoration occurred. It began and ended within a week. The Republic was resurrected and the government reestablished. But the lack of cooperation between the central and the provincial governments continued, hindering the smooth functioning of their respective fiscal administrative organizations. This situation still prevails today. The present movement for the restoration of tariff autonomy, however, marks the beginning of a new era in the fiscal history of the Chinese Republic, namely, the stage of reconstruction.

This in brief is the story of China's fiscal development under the Republican régime. Many mistakes were committed in these few years. We shall consider now a few of the most outstanding of these, which the government should exercise its utmost care to avoid in the future:

(a) *The Foreign Control of the Salt Tax.*—As we have seen, Yuan Shih-kai obtained a " Reorganization Loan " from the foreign bankers in 1913. The amount of that loan was £25,000,000. As security he pledged the salt tax, which was thus placed under foreign supervision. According to the agreement made, China was also required to employ foreign advisers in the bureaus of Auditing and National Loans. The national government also suffered a great loss in that £4,000,000 was deducted from the loan as commission, etc. for the banking groups of the foreign nations concerned.

(b) *The Secret Japanese Loans.*—According to a noted authority [1] on Far Eastern affairs, Japan lent only 17,670,-000 yen to the Chinese government between Jan. 1, 1909, and the outbreak of the World War, and 32,000,000 yen to the Hanyehping Iron and Steel Corporation. Whereas, from August, 1914, to Oct. 25, 1918, she lent no less than 391,-430,000 yen to the Peking government. Ostensibly these funds were for financing China's participation in the World War, but in practice they were used by the northern militarists to wage war against their political opponents, who formed a separate government in Canton. This ushered in a series of civil wars, which have not yet been completely suppressed. Most of the loans were secretly concluded while the Terauchi cabinet was in power in Japan. They were made with the vicious purpose of holding China under Japanese bondage. None of them was approved by the Chinese National Assembly, and the practice of making secret loans to the militarists in authority has been bitterly denounced by the Chinese people.

(c) *Forced Suspension of Specie Payments.*—To finance his monarchistic movement, Yuan Shih-kai forced the Bank of China and the Bank of Communications, two government banking institutions, to issue notes for which no cash reserve was provided. As a consequence, these two banks suspended specie payment, and the value of their notes in the Peking market dropped as low as to forty per cent of the face value. [2]

(d) *Undesirable Practices in the Floating of Domestic Loans.* — According to a statement made by the Chinese Financial Readjustment Commission, up to the spring of 1921, nine series of domestic-loan bonds had been issued by the central government under the Republican régime. They

---

[1] Millard, T. F., *Democracy and the Eastern Problem*, pp. 187-192.

[2] *Chinese Economic Monthly*, Peking, Oct., 1925.

STAGES OF FISCAL HISTORY

were the Patriotic Loan, the Eight Per Cent Military Loan, the First Year, the Third Year, the Fourth Year, the Fifth Year loans, the Seventh Year Short Term, the Seventh Year Long Term, and the Eighth Year Currency Reorganization loans. The total amount outstanding was approximately $315,000,000. Of these loans, only the Third Year, the Fourth Year, and the Seventh Year Short Term loans were secured with definite and reliable funds; the remainder were mostly unsecured or under-secured. The worst ones were quoted on the market at the outset of their issue at only twenty per cent of their face value.[1]

(e) *The Loss of the Right of Custody of Customs Revenue.*—Prior to the Revolution of 1911, the Customs revenue was deposited in the Chinese " customs banks." When the customs houses needed money to defray their expenses, they made application for funds to the Chinese authorities. The foreigners had never lodged any complaints against this system, because the Chinese government met promptly its foreign obligations for which the customs revenue was pledged. After the outbreak of the Revolution of 1911, the customs receipts were held by the provincial authorities of the provinces where customs houses were located. As a result, the customs banks were forced to close. On January 30, 1912, a temporary arrangement was made by China with the foreign creditor governments, providing that the Hongkong and Shanghai Banking Corporation, the Deutsch-Asiatic Bank, and the Russo-Asiatic Bank be made the custodians of the customs funds. After China's declaration of war against Germany and her cessation of diplomatic relations with Czarist Russia, this privilege was almost entirely monopolized by the Hongkong and Shanghai Banking Corporation. The Chinese banks have repeatedly demanded

[1] *Chinese Economic Monthly*, Peking, October, 1925; see also *Bankers' Weekly*, Shanghai, No. 391, March 24, 1925, pp. 42-43.

the abolition of this practice, but no satisfactory agreement has been arrived at up to the present. The significance of this problem has well been pointed out by Mr. T. S. Wei in a recent article.[1] He shows that the customs receipts constitute the most important single item of revenue of the national government in China. For the years 1923 and 1924 the annual customs receipts were 57 and 69 million Haikwan taels respectively; the sum represented by a year's receipts is greater than the amount of silver in circulation in the country. It is estimated that the amount of silver in circulation in the country is 70,000,000 silver dollars or 50,000,000 Haikwan taels. In order to control the financial resources of the country the custody of this immense fund should be restored to the government bank of China.

(f) *The Abandonment of the Practice of Budget-Making and the Ineffectiveness of the Auditing System.*—Under the Republican régime, two national budgets were made; one in 1915, and one in 1919, but only the earlier one was enforced. Owing to the internal political disturbances, no attempt has been made to prepare a national budget since 1919. The only reliable information regarding the present Chinese fiscal conditions to be had at this time is a rough estimate which has been worked out by the Chinese Financial Readjustment Commission.[2] According to this estimate, the approximate amounts of national revenue and expenditure may be tabulated as follows:

[1] Wei, T. S., "Chinese Banks Should Hold the Customs Deposits," Special Tariff Conference Issue, *China Weekly Review*, Nov. 1, 1925, pp. 25, 26 and 28.

[2] China's Finances under the Republican Régime, *Chinese Economic Monthly*, October, 1925.

I. NATIONAL REVENUES:

    (A) Revenues collected by the offices under the direct supervision of the central government: Customs and salt revenues, wine and tobacco taxes, stamp duties, revenue from government property, receipts of central government offices $280,437,696

    (B) Central government revenues assigned to, and disposed of by, the provincial governments: Land tax, *likin*, miscellaneous taxes, revenue from government industries in the provinces, and miscellaneous receipts 179,522,438

        Total $459,960,134

II. NATIONAL EXPENDITURES:

    (A) Administrative expenses $168,359,865
    (B) Amount required to meet loans 173,274,337
    (C) Military expenditures 274,862,058

        Total $616,496,260

As most provinces do not regularly report their accounts to the central government, no complete, accurate statement of government revenue and expenditure can be secured. The revenues listed above are theoretical rather than actual. The entire customs revenue is pledged as security for loans and indemnities, and the surplus of the salt revenue, i. e., the balance of this revenue after the deduction of the sum for the payment of interest and principal on foreign loans for which this source of revenue is pledged, is usually retained by the provincial authorities. The central government can have, to meet its expenses, only that portion of the revenue which is not retained by the provinces. It has been recently reported that the central government received in 1924 only about a million dollars silver of the total receipts of 40 million dollars silver from the wine and tobacco taxes, and about 300,000 dollars silver from the stamp duties. As a result of these pledges and retentions, only about one-tenth of the total revenues listed was actually received by the central government. Whereas the amounts of expenditure listed are the sums actually needed to run the government, to pay off its debts, or to supply the funds demanded by the selfish militarists to maintain their superfluous armies.

It may also be noted that the item for military expenditure does not represent the actual amount spent, for most of the so-called national armies are supported by the provinces where they are stationed, and their accounts are not reported to the central government. Moreover, owing to the urgent demand of the militarists, military expenses usually receive first consideration, while administrative expenses are neglected. The wretched condition of the civil administrative organizations may be shown by merely mentioning the fact that the teachers in the government universities, the judges, and the personnel of some of the departments of the central government have been compelled to strike for their back pay, and that the fiscal ministers have to appropriate not only funds to meet current expenses, but also arrears which the government owes to its civil servants.

But even as it stands, the amount shows that the military expenditure approximates 45 per cent of the total expenditure and almost 60 per cent of the total revenue. Administrative expenditures, on the other hand, constitute only 27 per cent of the total revenue. The remaining 28 per cent is required to meet payment of interest and principal on various loans, including well-secured domestic and foreign loans, interest due on unsecured foreign loans, loans with amortization provision, short-term loans from Chinese banks, treasury notes, and other bank advances.

At first glance, the annual deficit would appear to be only 156,536,126 dollars silver, but since the figures representing government revenues are not actual but merely theoretical, the real deficit is much larger than that given.

The only paying public industry of the national government is the post-office.[1] In 1924 the revenue of this department was $23,000,000 silver, and the working expenses about $19,000.000 silver. The government railways are unable to pay either the interest or the principal of the foreign loans contracted for their construction, because of the retention of the railways revenues by the militarists, and the government telegraph is losing money every year through the failure of the central and provincial governments to pay for telegraph service.[2]

Laws regarding government accounting and the auditing of government accounts were promulgated in 1915, but, owing to the neglect of budget-making and to the failure of the militarists and the corrupt civil officers to report expenditures, these laws have never been effectively put into force. For this reason, no complete national fiscal reports have been compiled since the establishment of the present Republic.

Some Constructive Fiscal Measures Considered.—In spite of the fact that fiscal development under the Republic has not come up to the expectation of the Chinese people, certain progress has been made which is worth mention. First, except in the provinces of Kansu and Sinkiang, the custom of paying land taxes in kind was abolished in 1912,[3] and the much-abused system of transporting grain from certain rice-producing provinces to the national capital by the incompetent officials instead of competitive merchants was thus done away with. Second, in some localities, the surveying of land for the assessment of taxes under the leadership of the gentry was successfully carried out, and this warrants

---

[1] For the development of the Chinese postal revenues, see *China Year Book 1924-1925*, edited by H. G. Woodhead, Tientsin Press, p. 410.

[2] *Bankers' Weekly,* Shanghai, No. 391, March 24, 1925, pp. 55-64.

[3] Chia, S. Y., *op. cit.,* pp. 267-279.

the hope that, when the national government becomes more stable, the reform measures of land taxation, as first suggested by Robert Hart and elaborated by the Bureau of Land Measurement and other experts, will be put into practice.[1]   Third, the salt tax administration, with the aid of foreign experts, has been much improved, and the salt tax has been more or less successfully transformed from a provincial revenue into a national revenue.   Fourth, the tobacco and wine taxes have given promise of fiscal success,[3] and will be good substitutes for the salt tax when the latter is abolished.   Fifth, the experimental separation of central and provincial revenues under the régime of Yuan Shih-kai has fairly demonstrated that such separation is quite feasible, although his over-centralization policy did China more harm than good and is no longer tolerated by the Chinese people. Sixth and last, the recent movements for the restoration of tariff autonomy and the abolition of *likin* have aroused a profound interest and enthusiasm among the general public for the thorough reform of domestic taxation and customs duties.

On Oct. 23, 1925, the Financial Rehabilitation Conference, headed by Dr. W. W. Yen, adopted a general program[2] for the reform of domestic taxation, the restoration of customs tariff, and the readjustment of the existing system of the maritime customs administration.   Article I of the program stated that the Chinese government, acting on the principle that the power of taxation is the prerogative of a sovereign state, shall exercise the power of tariff autonomy.   All existing treaty stipulations, and all notes or statements exchanged between China and the Powers which infringe upon the aforesaid principle shall be revised according

[1] Huang, H. L., *Land Tax in China*, pp. 145-172.

[2] Chia, S. Y., *op. cit.*, pp. 542-613.

[3] *China Weekly Review*, Shanghai, Dec. 12, 1925, p. 44.

to Articles II, III, IV, V, VI, and VII of this program. These articles may be regrouped into two, namely, constructive measures relating to domestic taxation and constructive measures relating to the customs.

(A) *Constructive Measures relating to Domestic Taxation.*—These measures may be summarized as follows:

1. *Thorough reform of domestic taxation.* — All existing treaty stipulations relative to domestic taxation, such as produce tax, consumption tax, and excise are forthwith declared abrogated. All regulations concerning domestic taxes shall hereafter be determined by the Chinese government (Art. II).

2. *Abolition of likin and the uniform taxation of Chinese citizens and alien residents.*—The Chinese government voluntarily undertakes to abolish *likin*, native customs duties, reimport taxes, transit dues and all other miscellaneous duties which are in the nature of the domestic transit duties. All people domiciled within the territory of the Republic of China, irrespective of their nationalities, shall hereafter be subject to the payment of taxes in accordance with the Chinese domestic tax regulations (Art. III).

At the committee meeting of the Special Tariff Conference held at Peking, on November 3, 1925, Dr. C. T. Wang made the following declaration on behalf of the Chinese government:

There is no greater detriment to the economic development of China than the *likin* system. . . . The Chinese people have for years been clamoring for the abolition of this tax, and to this end the central government has created a Financial Rehabilitation Commission composed of representatives of the military and civil authorities of the whole country. After mature consideration it has been decided to abolish the *likin* system, so that the economic welfare of the people may be advanced, foreign commerce benefited, the foundations of national finance firmly established, and the international relations of the country strengthened.

The Chinese government therefore declares that the abolition of *likin* will be completely carried out not later than the first day of the first month of the 18th year of the Republic (1929).

As the *likin* has long constituted one of the main sources of the revenue of provincial governments, and the total amount of its annual yield has been as great as seventy million silver dollars, Chinese currency, the central government is undertaking to provide in advance a special fund to compensate the provinces for the loss of this revenue. Out of the fund each province will receive its quota according to the annual deficit which it incurs through the abolition of *likin*. For the adjustment of this matter two different periods are proposed. During the first period, a portion of the customs revenue derived from the increased rates above the five per cent on imports, is to be appropriated for compensation. During the second period, when tariff autonomy is put into effect, appropriation is to be made out of the customs revenue. By the end of December, 1928, the plan for the abolition of *likin* will be completely executed.

At the same conference, Dr. C. T. Wang stated the determination of the Chinese government to tax foreigners residing in any settlement or treaty port, declaring that the present exemptions enjoyed by foreigners are the outcome of the unjustifiable treaties. This settled national policy shows the necessity for the revision of the treaties in which China had committed herself with regard to the question of extraterritoriality.

(B) *Constructive Measures relating to Customs.*—The measures advocated for the reform of the customs were as follows:

1. *Reform of Export Tariff.*—The Chinese government shall

fix the export tariff rates, which shall be regulated with reference to the kind, quality and the condition of production and consumption of the goods exported (Art. IV).

2. *Reform of Import Tariff.*—The import duties shall be classified according to the kind and quality of the goods imported and in accordance with the provisions of the customs schedules: but in case of certain kinds of goods coming from nations with whom China has Agreements of Reciprocity the tariff rates shall be determined by the said agreements (Art. V).

3. *Special regulation for wine, tobacco and other commodities monopolized by the government.*—The tariff for imported goods which fall under the Special Laws of the Republic of China, such as wine and tobacco and other government Monopolies, shall be determined by the aforesaid Laws (Art. VI).

4. *Periodical Revision of Tariff Schedules.*—The import and export tariff schedules shall be fixed by the Chinese government and revised from time to time following periodical investigation of the prices of goods.

In accordance with the general principles quoted above, the Chinese government promulgated a general customs tariff law [1] on October 24, 1925; the most important provisions are as follows:

1. *Provision for fixing the maximum rate of import duty.*— Except in the case of tobacco, wine and articles similar in nature to those under government monopoly, which shall be otherwise provided for,[2] the highest rate of import duty shall be 40 per cent and the lowest 7½ per cent (Art. 2).

2. *Provision regulating specific duty.*—The duty-paying value of goods subject to a specific duty shall be fixed, converted or adjusted on the basis of their average prices during the preceeding year (Art. 3).

---

[1] *China Weekly Review*, Shanghai, Nov. 7, 1925, p. 229.

[2] Article II of the law regulating the import duty on tobacco and wine, promulgated on the same date (Oct. 24, 1925), provided that the import duty on tobacco and wine shall range from 50 to 80 per cent *ad valorem*.

3. *Provision regulating ad valorem duty.*—The duty-paying value of goods subject to an *ad valorem* duty shall be fixed on the basis of their wholesale prices prevailing at the port of entry (Art. 4).

4. *Provision for reciprocity.*—In the event that an agreement exists with any country on terms of reciprocity with regard to the import duty of certain articles, the duty on these articles shall be in accordance with that agreement (Art. 5).

5. *Provision for retaliation.*—In the event that any country subjects Chinese articles to less favorable treatment than those of other countries, the government may by mandate impose an import duty on articles from that country in addition to the duty prescribed in the tariff, such increase of duty not to exceed in amount the value of such articles (Art. 6).

6. *Anti-bounty provision.*—In the event that a country grants an export bounty on its articles, the government may by mandate impose an import duty on such goods of the same amount as the said bounty, in addition to the duties prescribed in the tariff (Art. 7).

7. *Anti-dumping provision.*—In the event that the prices of foreign articles are intentionally and unreasonably lowered to such an extent that the government considers this a disturbance to the market, it may by mandate impose a duty commensurate with the proper prices, in addition to the duties prescribed in the tariff (Art. 8).

(C) *Constructive Program for the Readjustment of the Existing Maritime Customs Administration.*—In Article VIII of the general program mentioned above, the Financial Rehabilitation Commission further recommended that in pursuance of the principle of administrative integrity, the Chinese government shall have the right to readjust the existing Maritime Customs system. The state of affairs existing in this system was well pointed out by Dr. Wellington Koo in the Washington Conference as follows:—

Though the present system of administration (of the Chinese

customs) had been in existence for nearly 60 years, very few Chinese had been trained by that service. Out of 44 commissioners of customs, distributed among the treaty ports, he was not aware of a single post being at present occupied by a Chinese.[1]

In order to satisfy the legitimate nationalistic aspirations of the people and to restore to China her administrative integrity, the Maritime Customs Service must be made an institution national in character. The control of this service must be solely in the hands of the Chinese people.

From the above brief survey of the fiscal history of the Chinese Republic, we see that the causes of the fiscal disorganization of the country are four in number. The first two may be called the external causes of the fiscal chaos; they are the bondage of the unequal and unjustifiable treaties relating to the tariff restrictions and the exemption of the alien residents in China from taxation. Both these restrictions have contributed immeasurably to the fiscal difficulties of the present Republic. The third and fourth causes are of internal origin. They are the destruction by the military autocracy existing in China throughout the last decade of the necessary requirements of a modern fiscal machinery, namely, the administrative, judicial, and legislative control of budget-making, accounting, reporting, and the proper handling of the responsible officers; and the lack of democratic fiscal statesmanship, which has made the Republic the prey of a host of selfish, greedy and unprincipled ministers of public finance, who were contented to be the cashiers of militarists rather than of the people at large.

It is evident, therefore, that unless some underlying principles for a democratic constructive fiscal program are formulated, no proper re-distribution of political power between the

[1] Willoughby, W. W., *China at the Conference*, pp. 105-106.

national and local governments can be made, nor will it be possible to find a scientific and lasting solution for all the pending difficult fiscal problems which confront China today. If this diagnosis is correct, a study of fiscal ideals from both the theoretical and the practical points of view is necessary.

PART THREE

Fiscal Reforms and the Future of Chinese Democracy

SINCE political reorganization is one of the prerequisites of China's fiscal reconstruction, it is evident that the success of the latter depends largely upon that of the former. Although China has been a republic for nearly fifteen years, her problems of constitutional as well as administrative reform remain unsolved. This shows that the fundamental difficulty which the country has to face at present is political. But it is also true that China cannot accomplish any substantial governmental reform unless she takes definite steps to solve the delicate and pressing fiscal problems confronting her today.

The political institutions as developed in China are admittedly different from those of the western countries. The Chinese people, however, are trying to establish their government on the basis of their own political tradition and at the same time along the principles of modern democracy.

Notwithstanding that the general conception of democracy is rather vague, the definition given by Abraham Lincoln in his Gettysburg speech is most widely accepted. Availing ourselves of this clear-cut definition of popular government, we shall endeavor to formulate certain principles for the study of China's present-day fiscal problems under the following general headings: (1) Finance of the people and the democratic principles governing taxation and public indebtedness, (2) Finance by the people and the legislative control of budget, and (3) Finance for the people, with several

169

canons suggested as rules for the regulation of governmental expenditures.

I. FINANCE OF THE PEOPLE AND THE DEMOCRATIC PRINCIPLES GOVERNING TAXATION AND PUBLIC INDEBTEDNESS

Secretary Mellon has well said, " Taxation is the people's business." [1] So also is public indebtedness. But in China unfortunately the people have little voice in these matters. As mentioned before, the causes of China's present fiscal difficulties are both external and internal. The imposition, from without, of unjust treaty stipulations has deprived her of the powers of tariff autonomy and of levying taxes upon foreigners as well as upon Chinese, whether individuals or corporations, having legal residences in the so-called treaty ports. Internally, the subordination of civil authorities to the autocratic military chieftains has placed the national finance at the mercy of a host of unscrupulous, selfish, war-like militarist-politicians. To remedy these outstanding evils, the following ideals must be realized:

(a) *Fiscal Autonomy in Place of Fiscal Restriction.*— In spite of the fact that a conventional tariff does not necessarily prove harmful to either of the parties concerned in a tariff treaty, the unilateral most-favored-nation treatment accorded to other nations by China and the unreasonably low and uniform customs rate of 5 per cent on both imports and exports have undoubtedly resulted in an enormous loss of revenue to the Chinese government and in the decline of China's international trade.

With tariff autonomy restored, there come the problems of choice between a tariff for revenue or for protection, between a tariff based on reciprocity or on retaliation, between one based on specific duties or on *ad valorem* duties. If a

[1] Mellon, A. W., *Taxation: The People's Business*, New York, 1925, *passim.*

protective tariff were adopted, the questions would arise as to how high the tariff wall should be, and how the varying costs of production at home and abroad might be ascertained and compared in order that a sufficiently high rate of import duty might be levied on foreign goods to give just protection to the infant industries at home.   Moreover, to prevent the dumping of goods into the Chinese market, now practiced by foreign merchants, and to counterbalance the bounties or subsidies given by foreign governments to their merchants trading in China, the anti-dumping and anti-bounty provisions of the Chinese National Tariff Law, promulgated on Oct. 26, 1925, should be strictly enforced.   As regards the export duty, the problem will simply be that of gradual reduction and complete abolition at the earliest possible date.

When we come to consider the principle of administrative integrity, the necessity for the readjustment of the existing system of customs administration will become self-evident. The problem of the retention of the foreigners now employed in the customs service should be determined according to the principle of administrative efficiency.

(b) *Civil Control as opposed to Military Control.*—As Mr. C. S. Chang, director of the Chinese National Institute of Political Science, has pointed out, unless the Chinese government is able to stop the usurpation of fiscal powers by the military chieftains, any discussion of centralization or decentralization will be futile.[1]   Therefore, for the sake of fundamental fiscal reorganization, three necessary steps must be taken: *first,* the establishment of peace throughout the nation; *second,* the subordination of military power to civil power; and, *third,* the separation, and at the same time the coordination, of functions between the national and the provincial governments.   It is only through these steps that the

[1] Chang, Car Sun, *A Memorandum on the Chinese National Constitution,* p. 104.

separation of central and local expenditures and revenues
can be put into effect, and the program for political reorganization and fiscal reconstruction be carried out.

(c) *Finance by Taxation instead of Finance by Loans.*—
In discussing the question of deficit financing, Professor H.
C. Adams stated that unless the demands of the government
for money are just, neither a loan nor a tax is capable of defence.[1] If we bear this proposition in mind and proceed to
examine the fiscal history of the Chinese Republic of the past
fourteen years, we shall agree that the sums wasted in waging
civil wars are absolutely unjustifiable. Even admitting that,
during a period of this sort, in which the form of government was changed from absolute monarchy to constitutional
republic, public credit may be employed to cover running
expenses of short duration for the government concerned,
no one can defend the practice of reckless borrowing to meet
the greater part of regular administrative expenditures as
resorted to throughout the present régime. Therefore, if
Chinese finance is to be built on a sound basis, the principle
of meeting regular expenditures with regular revenue from
taxation should be strictly observed, and the policy regarding public indebtedness should be one similar to that established by Alexander Hamilton for the United States in the
early stage of American history, namely, " to give all possible
energy to public credit, by a firm adherence to its strictest
maxims; and yet to avoid the evils of an excessive employment of it by true economy and system in the public expenditures, by steadily cultivating peace, and by using sincere,
efficient and persevering endeavors to diminish present
debts, prevent the accumulation of new (debts) and secure
the discharge, within a reasonable period, of such as it may
be at any time a matter of necessity to contract. . . ." [2]

[1] Adams, H. C., *Public Debts*, pp. 77-78.

[2] *The Works of Alexander Hamilton*, Communication to the Senate on
Public Credit, Jan. 20, 1795, Henry Cabot Lodge's ed., 1904, vol. iii,
pp. 299-300.

(d) *Direct versus Indirect Taxation.*—In discussing the development of taxation, Professor Seligman has made it clear that, in democratic communities, where legislation is influenced by the mass of the people, we commonly discern a tendency to oppose indirect taxes.[1] In China, the land tax was long the chief revenue of the national government. The income derived from this source in the year 1753 was 37,660,000 silver taels, whereas the salt tax and the native customs duty, the two main items of indirect taxation at that time, yielded only 9,030,000 silver taels. In other words, the ratio between the yield of the direct and that of the indirect taxes was approximately 4 to 1.[2] This ratio remained relatively unchanged until the imposition of maritime customs in 1842 and the introduction of *likin* in 1853. Under the Republic, the revenues from the customs duties, the salt tax and the wine and tobacco taxes have been growing rapidly. According to the estimate made by the Chinese Ministry of Finance, the total amount of national revenue for the fiscal year 1925 was $459,960,134 silver, while the revenue from land taxes was only $88,286,226 silver.[3] This shows that the ratio of indirect to direct taxes is now approximately 5 to 1,[4] and that the main source of the revenue of the Chinese government today is the indirect, not the direct, tax. But indirect taxes are commonly burdensome and oppressive to the laboring class. And as soon as this class can make its voice heard, it will demand the abolition or reduction of the taxes on consumption and a general lessening of its burden.

[1] Seligman, E. R. A., *Essays in Taxation*, 1925, tenth ed., p. 7.

[2] Hu, C., *Chinese Fiscal History*, pp. 18-20.

[3] *Bankers' Weekly*, Shanghai, March 24, 1925, no. 391.

[4] Revenues from public industries, administrative and judicial fees, etc. were also included in the estimate of the total amount of national revenue, so that the ratio is one of other forms of revenue, mainly indirect taxes, to that derived from land tax.

Recommendations for the Reform of the Tax System.—
In formulating a program for the reform of the tax system,
special attention should be paid to the following factors:

(I) *Ethical Factors.*—The whole system of Chinese taxation should first be examined from the ethical point of view.
Any tax which violates the fundamental principles of fiscal
ethics should be abolished as speedily as possible, even though
it produces immense revenue for the government. For instance, the unjust tax on salt and certain other taxes on
necessities of life should be done away with as soon as sufficient revenue can be obtained by increases in the wine and
tobacco taxes to compensate for the loss of revenue which
this reform will entail. In other words, consumption taxes
should be limited to a few commodities, so chosen that necessary or healthful consumption will be either lightly taxed or
entirely exempt from the taxation and luxurious or harmful
consumption will be subject to taxation at higher rates.

As a means of realizing the ideal of justice in taxation,
capital value or net income, rather than gross rent or gross
produce, should be made the basis of the land and real estate
taxes, and a progressive tax on individual income should be
introduced. These propositions are sound in theory; but
when and how to put them into practice is a practical political and administrative problem.

(II) *Economic Factors.*—Next to the ethical considerations come those of economic justification. As the chief
economic problem of China today is production, such taxes
as export duties and internal transit duties, which greatly
hamper the development of national productive industries
and practically lead to economic suicide, should be abolished
at the earliest possible date, and their reinstatement under the
disguise of other names should be carefully guarded against.
For the sake of giving necessary and justifiable encouragement to infant industries and preventing these from being

destroyed by foreign competition, a moderate protective tariff is both defensible and advisable.

The over-burdened merchants should be relieved of the numerous oppressive and unjust taxes on their business; and a scientific and practicable system of business taxation based largely on gross, or even better on net, income, should be introduced. As modern transportation facilities develop, the value of land increases rapidly and steadily, especially that of commercial and industrial centers. In order to readjust the existing system of land taxation so as to conform to the needs of the changing economic condition, a general reassessment should be made, and a national survey and valuation should be prepared.

(III) *Sociological Factors.*—Since the Chinese fiscal system has a deep-rooted historical background, a new system of taxation should be introduced only after a careful consideration of its social effects. For example, the family system is the foundation of Chinese society. This has its merits and defects. The merits which concern the economic life of the nation are that it (1) fosters the spirit of cooperation among the members of the family and (2) maintains the solidarity of society. Its defects are that it (1) weakens the enterprising spirit of the younger members of a family, who live on the resources of their elders; (2) encourages the undesirable early marriages by allowing the young couples to rely upon the support of their families; and (3) overburdens the more capable members of society by imposing upon them the responsibility of providing for families of huge size.

To check the steady growth of oversized families and the accumulation of unduly large fortunes, the imposition of a progressive inheritance or estate tax is justifiable, although the amount of exemption should be reasonably liberal and the rate of taxation should be as moderate as possible, in order that the desire to save may not be discouraged, the invested capital not be disturbed, and the evil practices of evasion and fraud not be resorted to by the people.

(IV) *Regional Factors.*—Because of the existing differences in the tax systems of various provinces and localities, the Chinese scholars, though maintaining that certain general principles for the reform of land taxation should be observed by the taxing authorities, fully realize that any program for provincial or local tax reform can best be worked out by the province or locality concerned and, especially, that the land tax should be assessed and collected by the provincial governments instead of by the national government. As regards a protective tariff, the divergence of economic interests between the industrial centers and the rural districts demands careful consideration by both practical statesmen and theoretical economists.

(V) *Political Factors.*—As China proposes to adopt a federal form of government, the evils of double or multiple taxation should be prevented and a proper division of central and local taxation should be made so that the fiscal relations between the federal and the provincial and local governments may be kept harmonious and an ideal interprovincial comity be promoted and maintained.

(VI) *Administrative Factors.*—The canons of honesty, economy and efficiency in fiscal administration should be strictly observed. Tax collectors should not, through the abuse of their powers, promote their personal interests at the expense of the state or of the people, but should fulfil their duties honestly and efficiently, thereby gaining the respect of the people. It is a national calamity that the present fiscal offices in China have become so degraded that reputable citizens do not care to accept appointments to them. It is therefore the duty of every patriotic son of China to see that these public offices are made clean and kept clean.

For the purposes of economy and efficiency, the policy of consolidation of offices should be followed; the cost of tax collection should be reduced to the minimum; and expert advice should be enlisted for the sake of technical efficiency.

(VII) *Technical Factors.*—The tasks of attaining ideal justice in the distribution of taxation and increasing the efficiency of tax administration involve certain technical problems. The methods by which progressive rates of income tax have been worked out in various countries, such as Italy, the Australian Commonwealth and the United States, are full of interesting suggestions. The methods of property valuation for taxation purposes practiced in some of the leading American municipalities merit careful study. The technique of taxation is becoming more and more important, and efficient fiscal administration depends as much upon the valuable service of practical experts as upon the sound teachings of economic theorists.

With reference to China, the difficulty of administering such new taxes as income and inheritance taxes will be primarily a technical one, and the problems of educating the tax payers and training the tax administrators will arise when these taxes are put into operation.

We should always bear in mind that even a good tax law usually turns out to be a bad one if it is poorly administered. This was the case in the failure of Wang An-shih's fiscal experiments. It will also be the case if the new system of income tax is administered by a host of untrained or unprincipled fiscal officials or if provision is not made for such administrative, accounting, and other technical facilities as are necessary for the honest and efficient operation of the tax.

(VIII) *Psychological Factors.*—The fundamental problem of fiscal reform, however, centers in the necessity of removing certain misconceptions regarding taxation; chief among these are the following:

(a) *Taxation as Tribute.*—The popular conception of taxation among the Chinese people today is still a traditional one, that is, they believe that a tax is paid to the government in order to avoid extortion by those in authority; they do not expect the government to confer any benefit upon them in return for their contributions. For this reason, they do not care much about how the government spends their money, but only ask that it take as little of this money as possible. In other words, they still consider taxation as tribute, not realizing that to pay taxes is the civic duty of a citizen who has a voice regarding these taxes, and what shall be done with the proceeds, while tribute is an imposition laid by a sovereign upon his subjects who have no voice in the matter. That is to say, they have not yet so far understood the fundamental principles of democratic taxation, but are still clinging to the old conception of tribute which had existed throughout the monarchical period of Chinese history. This shows that the fiscal beliefs of a people once acquired can not easily be changed.

(b) *Indirect Taxes Regarded as Preferable to Direct Taxes.*—Another noteworthy point is that the Chinese people are more favorable to indirect than to direct taxes. This fiscal psychology owes its origin to the school of the Jurists who established the policy of indirect taxation in the Chinese tax system in the form of iron and salt monopolies. The increase of the land tax seven times within a period of twenty-one years(1618-1639 A. D.), which brought the Ming dynasty to a downfall, also helped to strengthen this antagonism to direct taxes. Popular opposition to any increase in the land tax is, then, very strong, and monopolistic policies are regarded as preferable. In this the Chinese people exhibit a fiscal psychology similar to that of the French. The explanation of this attitude is simply that they do not feel the burden of indirect taxation so long as the rates of the taxes are reasonable.

(c) *Minimum Taxation as Best Taxation.*—The third popular misconception is that the minimum taxation is the best taxation. This is largely due to the profound influence of Lao Tzŭ's philosophy of least government. As a matter of fact, the so-called minimum taxation does not necessarily prove to be really the minimum at all. In his special correspondence to *The New York Times,* Mr. Thomas F. Millard has drawn us the following true, although unpleasant, picture of the fiscal conditions in China today:

" It has been said that revolutions start with the tax collector. Taxation may bring about the completion of the revolution in China. Taxes may be the straw which finally will break down the patience of the Chinese under the present misrule and enable them to throw off political inertia and get rid of officials who exploit them. . . .

" Regarded one way, the Chinese are taxed more lightly, probably, than any other civilized people in the world. That statement, however, must be qualified at once, for taxation in China has two forms—legitimate and illegitimate.

" Legitimate taxation in China is so small that it would be the envy of other nations, provided the tale ended there. Take a few figures recently compiled by a foreign fiscal expert. In 1922 the annual per capita revenue derived from taxes and duties in the following countries, in silver dollars, amounted to:

Great Britain	$170.00
France	90.00
United States (Federal Taxes only)	120.00
Belgium	30.00

" It is plain that taxes put in terms of money do not represent accurately the true measure of the burden on a people who pay them; for this depends on living standards and average earnings. A better comparison is had by turning to Oriental countries near to China, whose annual per capita tax figures in silver dollars are:

Japan	$16.00
Philippines	7.50
Indo-China	5.50
Siam	9.50
Dutch Indies	15.00
China	1.20

" Of legitimate taxes the Chinese, therefore, pay one-fifth of the average taxation paid in French Indo-China and one-eighth of the average paid in Siam. Yet the population is more frugal and industrious than those peoples, and the country has more resources than those regions. The Chinese pay one-twelfth of the legitimate taxation that the Japanese pay. . . .

" So while legitimate taxation in China always, in comparison with other countries, has been ridiculously low, other forms of taxation raised the average to the level of normality, which here, as elsewhere, is all the people can be induced or compelled to pay.

" In so far as the Chinese masses suffer today from fiscal oppression it is from the kind of taxes which are irregular and unaccounted for. This illegitimate taxation can be summarized under these headings; arbitrary levies on business and on property, special and variable duties and transit charges, diversion of railway revenues, confiscation, depreciated and worthless currencies and other methods which can be called extortion. . . .

"A theory which is held by most of the Chinese intelligentsia is that the Chinese masses and the middle class will never comprehend their modern relation to government except by suffering under the malfeasance and failures. Those Chinese are inclined to believe that the worse this condition becomes the sooner it will bring about reform.

" Therefore it is conceivable that China's ancient evil, official 'squeeze,' as applied through the tax collector, eventually will arouse among the people the spirit and the will to accomplish national reconstruction." [1]

Thus it may be said that, although the legitimate tax burden of the Chinese people is light, their ultra-burden of taxation is not a light one at all.

[1] *The New York Times*, April 4, 1926.

The misconception regarding the benefits of low taxation is existent of course in other countries also. Let us quote a passage from Mr. Sidney Webb's article *What about the Rates? or Municipal Finance and Municipal Autonomy,* in order to show how the tax payers' psychology may affect the development of a locality or municipality. The passage reads:

"What is it that today most hinders municipal progress? I am afraid that most elected persons would say that it is the rate-payers' fear of any increase in the burden of rates. It is this fear that damps the ardor and hinders the work of the enthusiastic reformer who has been elected to a town or district council. What is even more important, it is this very real feeling that strengthens the hands of those members of every council who are anyhow not enthusiastic for social change."

Then he continues:

" It seems to me inevitable that the electors should have to feel that, whenever any new or increased expenditure is to be incurred, it is they themselves who will have to pay. This is the price that we pay for local self-government. . . . We cannot have local autonomy without local finance."

This is an advice which the Chinese tax-payers of today should welcome.

Conclusions.—A program for the reform of Chinese taxation, then, must meet two requirements: (1) it must provide for the early reform of the old taxes and the successful introduction of new taxes in spite of the many technical and administrative difficulties involved; (2) it must arrange for the levying of direct taxation on the basis of income or capital value of property at the earliest possible moment, and for the gradual reduction and eventual abolition of

[1] *Fabian Tracts,* July, 1913, No. 172, pp. 2-3.

consumption taxes on the necessities of life as soon as the economic development of the country permits the introduction of better forms of taxation.

Fiscal scholars and administrators must bend every effort to educate the people regarding tax problems and to overcome the political, sociological, regional and psychological difficulties which lie in the way of fiscal reform. This policy of practical fiscal reforms to ameliorate the present wretched conditions can find its support in the following dialogue between Mencius and Tai Ying-chi, minister of the state of Sung:

Tai Ying-chi said to Mencius, " I am not able to get along at present by levying the tithe only, and cannot abolish the duties charged at the passes (i. e., customs houses) and in the markets. With your leave I will lighten, however, both the tax and the duties, until next year, and shall then make an end of them. What do you think of such a course?"

Mencius said, " Here is a man who every day appropriates some of his neighbor's strayed fowls. Some one says to him, ' Such is not the way of a good man; ' and he replies, ' With your leave I shall diminish my appropriations, and shall take only one fowl a month, until next year when I will make an end of the practice.' "

" If you know that the thing is unrighteous, then use all dispatch in putting an end to it; why wait until next year? " [1]

II. FINANCE BY THE PEOPLE AND THE LEGISLATIVE CONTROL OF THE BUDGET

Popular control of the public purse is the most effective safeguard of democratic government. The discontinuance of national budget-making since 1919 is an evidence of the lack of democratic control in Chinese finance: In order to establish the government on a true democratic basis, the following three fundamental principles should be observed.

[1] *Works of Mencius*, bk. iii, pt. ii, ch. viii.

(a) *Taxation with Representation.*—The principle, " No representation, no taxation," won for the propertied class their right to participate in the problems of taxation. As democracy advanced, the non-propertied class too demanded a voice in formulating the policies relating to government revenues and expenditures. Therefore, the principle of representation with taxation has been somewhat broadened into a principle of democratic finance with democratic representation.

Owing to the fact that representative government on a national scale is a new experiment in China, it is too early to pass judgment on the success of the system. Moreover, the present political turmoil is not due to the lack of a representative form of government, but to the lack of true representation of the public interests. Since the Chinese people have been successful for centuries with their guild and village self-government, we may safely say that they will not fail in the field of national self-government. The present system of regional representation, however, should be supplemented with group or occupational representation, because public interests in China can best be represented by cultural and economic groups organized to suit the national political ideals and traditions. With the public interests truly represented, we may expect that popular control of Chinese finance will become a reality.

(b) *Publicity of Accounts with Strict Enforcement of Administrative Responsibility.*—Ideal government requires both popular participation and efficient administration, because efficiency without popular participation usually results in dictatorship or autocracy, whereas participation without efficient administration inevitably leads to a reckless extravagance.

The Chinese people demand publicity of accounts from their national, provincial, and local governments. This movement indicates that fiscal secrecy, the source of various corrupt practices, can no longer be tolerated. But publicity is only one of the elements of democratic finance; at the same time, the administrative and judicial control of budget should be made effective and fiscal officers should be held strictly responsible by law. Due punishment should be inflicted upon those officers found guilty of graft or other dishonesty. The fiscal disorder of China today is due as much to want of administrative responsibility and to the freedom of corrupt officials from punishment as to lack of popular participation in the government.

(c) *Efficient Budget-Making with the Aid of Scientific Accounting.*—It is generally held by the fiscal scientists that the preparation of a budget should be entrusted to the executive departments and should be centralized in the treasury department or in an independent budget bureau. In order to facilitate the procedure of budget-making, to locate the definite administrative responsibility, and to help the general public to form a sound judgment upon public policy and administrative efficiency, a proper classification of public revenues and public expenditures is an absolute necessity. In former times, students of fiscal science attempted to measure the efficiency of governmental administration by comparing the tax burden of one country with that of another country or the expenditure of one locality with that of another. They are now trying to devise some more exact means of measurement, and to this end also, the proper classification of governmental receipts and expenditures is essential.

The classification of public expenditures should not only be logical, but useful in practice. *First,* according to the regularity or frequency of the occurrence of the specific item of government expenditure, the usual classification of public expenditure into ordinary and extraordinary expenditures can be made.   This is still worthy of being retained for the simple reason that the principle of meeting ordinary expenditure with ordinary revenue and extraordinary expenditure with extraordinary revenue may thus be employed with advantage.   *Second*, the classification of governmental expenditure may be undertaken from the standpoint of the nature of the funds provided for meeting the general or specific requirement of a government, and accounts may be so kept and reports so made that the revenues and expenditures on account of each fund, either general or special, can be definitely determined.   *Third*, from the standpoint of organization units, care should be taken to list all the divisions and subdivisions of the government in their proper relations of superiority, co-ordination or subordination, since the purposes of the classification of public expenditure are to show the line of authority as well as to ascertain the precise cost of maintaining and operating each unit of governmental organization.   *Fourth*, in view of the differentiation of governmental activities, it is necessary and at the same time advisable to separate general or institutional activities from specific or functional activities.   By means of this classification, we can easily see what amount it is proposed to devote to the protection of the country against foreign aggression, internal disorder, and other existing social evils such as crimes or the like, what amount to the promotion of education and scientific research, what amount to the protection of public health, what amount to the economic development of the country, and what is the total cost to the government for the promotion of public welfare in general.   *Fifth*, data must be obtained regarding the character or purpose of governmental outlays : that is, how much is to go (1) for capital outlay; (2) for fixed charges; and (3) for current expenses. *Finally*, expenditures should be classified by uses or objects; that is, the amount to be used for personal services, the amount for services other than personal, such as travel, freight and express, telephone, telegraph, printing, postage, etc., and the amount for maintenance, insurance, or materials purchased by the government. This classification serves to throw light upon such problems as personnel administration, the application of business methods in governmental administration, the efficiency of government purchasing, and the standards of property maintenance.[1] In short, a budget is not mere arithmetic; it is an expression of the will of the government as well as that of the people. It requires an integrated administrative system for its successful operation. It shows the working capacity of the body politic and at the same time the needs, the wastes, and, all in all, the physiological conditions of the government as a whole.

Although the measurement of governmental efficiency is still an experiment of recent origin, some of the methods devised for this purpose are worth noting. Recently accountants, administrators and others have established units of work for some governmental activities and have determined the unit costs of such work. In some instances they have attempted to determine the rate of work and to set standards of working efficiency thereby. To wit, the Reclamation Service of the United States government has not only worked out an elaborate system of expenditure accounts and cost accounts, but its reports made monthly, quarterly and annually carry definite unit costs, thus providing standards for judging as to economy or efficiency on a basis of past experience.[2] This shows that the principle of cost accounting may be introduced into the management of government, as well as business, affairs.

[1] *Cf.* Willoughby, W. F., *The Problem of a National Budget*, pp. 10-28 and 169-179.

[2] Metz Fund Handbooks of City Business: *A Handbook of Municipal Accounting*, ch. vi.

(d) *Effective Control of the Budget with Enlightened Public Opinion.*—As the fiscal problems of modern times are becoming more and more complicated, the people can not exercise their power of fiscal control intelligently unless they are well informed. For this reason, the tax laws and the like should be made as simple as possible. All information on these matters should be put into concise and intelligible form and should be freely and widely distributed by the government as a necessary aid for the universal diffusion of democratic fiscal education. Above all, popular interest in public finance should always be kept alive. It is generally believed that eternal vigilance is the price of liberty. It is also true that constant careful study of fiscal problems on the part of the citizens is one of the supreme requisites of citizenship. In China, the lack of popular interest in fiscal problems has long been a cause of political degradation. Special efforts should, therefore, be made to stimulate such interest and so to enlighten, strengthen and organize public opinion that it will be able to deal properly and effectively with the fiscal problems which may arise from time to time in the national, provincial, or local governments.

III. FINANCE FOR THE PEOPLE AND THE CANONS GOVERNING PUBLIC EXPENDITURES

No public expenditure is justifiable unless it is employed directly or indirectly for the promotion of general welfare. The term welfare is, however, just as ambiguous as the term justice. Many views on welfare are presented. The Confucians held that ethical culture is the root of human happiness, while the Jurists maintained that economic prosperity is the basis of ethical culture. Turning to the modern economic philosophers, we find the same diverse opinions. John Ruskin said: " That country is the richest which nourishes the greatest number of noble and happy human beings." [1]   Whereas Karl Marx, stressing the side of material well-being, maintained that " the method of production in material existence conditions social, political and mental evolution in general." [2]   Both arguments emphasize the extreme, yet contain a certain amount of truth.   As practical experience shows, ethical culture and material prosperity are both necessary for the attainment of maximum social welfare.   Now, let us discuss some fundamental problems of great fiscal and social importance.

(a) *Finance for War or for Peace.*—The cost of armament has long been regarded as the leading and most necessary item of public expenditure.   This is a natural and inevitable result of militaristic nationalism.   But it will be seen to be an abnormal, rather than a normal, fiscal condition if we take into consideration the whole course of human history.   Sir Josiah Stamp has emphatically pointed out that " one of the most important historical reasons for the rapid economic development of the American continent is that it has been able to develop its resources as a unified whole instead of being split up into a large number of separate military areas " and that " one may get an indication of the economic advantages of the absence of armaments by reflecting on what the position of the United States would have been industrially, or economically, if a large army for each side, with a whole line of boundary forts, had had to be maintained at the national expense of each country on both the Canadian and the United States side of that boundary of thousands of miles extent." [3]   This he has called a present-day example of the benefit of non-militaristic development.

[1] " Unto This Last ": Four Essays on the First Principles of Political Economy, p. 125.

[2] *Zur Kritik der Politischen Oekonomie*, Erstes Heft (1859), pp. iv, v; Seligman, *Economic Interpretation of History*, p. 44.

[3] Stamp, J. C., *Studies in Current Problems in Finance and Government*, pp. 86-87.

When we come to consider the development of Chinese polity, we find that, in the Constitution of the Chou dynasty, a dynasty popularly known as the zenith of Chinese cultural development in the ancient period, the military expenditure was placed in the eighth place, just preceding the last item of public expenditure, viz., the temporary or extraordinary expenditure for donations or gifts by the emperor, but following such items as expenditures for worship, diplomatic entertainment, famine relief, public works, etc., etc.[1] In other words, military expenditure was considered the last, rather than the first, item of regular national expenditure. At that time, the functions of the central government consisted of six groups, namely, (1) general and fiscal administration, (2) administration for the distribution of public land and for the maintenance of the public educational system, (3) administration of religious rites, (4) military administration, (5) administration of justice, and (6) administration of public works and of labor.[2] This functional classification of governmental organization shows that much emphasis was laid upon the preparation for peace, not for war. Throughout the Chou dynasty, external and internal peace was maintained by a system of militia. This historical fact is another example of the practicability and advisability of the peaceful or non-militaristic development of a nation.

It is, however, obvious, as Professor John Dewey tells us, that "anything interwoven as war is with tradition, national histories, politics, economics, diplomacy and education must be approached from many angles."[3] What a fiscal scholar ought to emphasize is that the economic loss to the whole society through armament is not only the direct expenditure

[1] *Supra*, pp. 69-70.

[2] *Supra*, p. 67.

[3] Dewey, J., "What Outlawry of War Is Not," *The New Republic*, October 3, 1923, p. 149.

for war or for preparation for war, but also the check upon the national productive output resulting from the maintenance of men under arms who might otherwise be engaged in industry; not only the direct waste of human lives in the battlefields, but also the indirect waste of vital wealth in society at large, especially the members of the families of the deceased or disabled soldiers and those who are engaged in war industries; not only a destruction of the invaluable supply of natural resources for the purpose of armament, but also a destruction of the cultural products of nations; and, above all, not only a wicked prodigality of social wealth which the past generations have created, accumulated and saved, but also the imposition of a heavy fiscal burden upon the generations of the future for the financing of wars that are largely unjustifiable. It should be emphasized also that just as the evil effects of high taxation, such as resulted from the competitive armament and the World War, are cumulative, as Sir Josiah Stamp puts it,[1] the actual and potential economic benefits which would result from disarmament or reduction of armament would also be cumulative and progressive. And the expenditure for economic and cultural purposes may be properly called productive, reproductive, or sometimes even multi-productive.

Therefore, if the world is really to be made safe for democracy, or, we may say, if democracy is really to make the world safe for human development, the existing international injustices must be rectified; some honorable and effective means for settling international differences must be provided; armaments must be reduced to the lowest amount consistent with security; and preparation for peace, rather than for war, must become the leading topic of a constructive and normalized finance. We may call this the fiscal normality of a nation as well as of the whole world. Moreover,

---

[1] Stamp, J. C., *op. cit.*, p. 82.

although international peace is, strictly speaking, not a fiscal problem, it is a problem of an extra-fiscal or ultra-fiscal nature. In the present stage of political development, unless this fundamental problem of international relationship can be properly solved, the fiscal condition of various nations will remain in a state of abnormality. This may be conveniently termed the international aspect of national finance in the modern world, and fiscal scholars of the new era in which we live can neither neglect it nor minimize it.

(b) *Government by Parsimony or by Wise Economy.*— The distinction between parsimony and wise economy made by several Chinese statesmen is worth quoting. Liu An said: " A great nation can not be governed with petty methods;" that is to say, great statesmen practice not parsimony, but wise economy. Chen Hung-maun said: " If a governmental enterprise is to be enduring, it should not be inadequately financed," meaning thereby that if the project is constructive and permanent, to spend millions of dollars on it is economical; but if it is unjustifiable, to spend one cent on it is wasteful. These statements serve to show that governmental economy should be judged not solely by the amount of expenditure, but by the purpose for which the money is spent as well.[1]

It is generally held that governmental administration can seldom be measured by commercial standards of economy and efficiency on account of existing evils such as overload of personnel, red tape and traditional extravagance. But as soon as the principle of business efficiency is highly developed and the public becomes cognizant of the lack of economy and efficiency in the management of government funds, a demand will eventually arise for the application of business methods and standards to governmental finance. For example, since 1910, the departments of the United States government have

[1] Shaw, K. W., *Elements of Fiscal Science*, Shanghai, 1925, p. 36.

been standardizing their purchases through the General Supply Committee.[1] The supplies, materials, equipment, etc., purchased by the government have been well classified, and standard specifications covering most of these items have been made in order to protect the government against articles of inferior quality.[2] A department known as the Bureau of Efficiency was created in 1916 for the purposes of establishing and maintaining the system of efficiency ratings, studying the needs of the several departments and independent offices with respect to personnel, and investigating the duplication of statistical and other work and the administrative methods employed in the various branches of government.[3] Progress has also been made along similar lines in some American states, counties and municipalities.[4] Therefore, we may say that the ideal of applying scientific principles of economy and efficiency in governmental administration will be realized when the spoils system in one form or another is eliminated, when civil service is placed upon the basis of merit, and when the governmental service becomes so well organized that the application of the principles of centralization and standardization will prove to be practicable and desirable here as they have been shown to be in the administration of large corporations.

(c) *The Operation of Government Industries according to the Principle of Maximum Revenue or of Maximum Welfare.*—According to Professor H. C. Adams, the commercial functions of a government, such as the post office and the government railway, "have nothing to do with the theory

[1] Thomas, Arthur G., *Principles of Government Purchasing*, Institute for Government Research, Washington, D. C., pp. 123-140.

[2] Thomas, A. G., *op. cit.*, pp. 123-140.

[3] Weber, G. A., *Organized Efforts for the Improvement of Methods of Administration in the United States*, Institute for Government Research, 1919, pp. 104-112.

[4] *Ibid.*, pp. 114-278.

of public expenditures." [1] Such a sweeping conclusion is rather questionable, for although the investments for these enterprises are usually remunerative, the receipts may prove to be insufficient to cover the costs of operation or expansion. Even admitting that they are run at a profit and that the income derived therefrom constitutes a source of revenue, the basis upon which the government is justified in investing a certain amount of money to create capital accounts for these industries should nevertheless be taken into consideration by any theorist in discussing governmental expenditures.

The question as to whether the operation of certain industries should be in the hands of private entrepreneurs subject to the regulation of the government or entirely in the hands of the state, is a vital one, and it can be solved only on the basis of the characteristics of the industry in question and of the relative advantages which can be expected from the operation by the state or by a private corporation. In other words, no definite policy can be followed; the advisability of state ownership or private ownership, of state operation or private operation, of industries depends upon whether the state can conduct such industries more efficiently and economically than private entrepreneurs or vice versa. In general, however, when the industry is one that greatly affects the public interest, the state should operate it for the benefit of the people. It may also be said that, as democracy advances, such industries as are of great public concern will most probably be conducted according to the principle of minimum cost with maximum welfare rather with maximum revenue. In China, however, special efforts should be made to guard against the undue expansion of the sphere of governmental industries, because the Chinese people strongly favor the policy of economic non-interference and state-operated industries in China have so far proved unsuccessful.

[1] Adams, H. C., *Science of Finance*, p. 81.

(d) *Expenditure for Constructive Social Development or for Social Amelioration.*—In his university lectures soon to be included in his *Principles of Fiscal Science,* Professor Seligman has shown us that the development of fiscal policies may be divided into four stages, namely, repressive, preventive, ameliorative, and constructive. It is needless to say that the constructive development of society should be the ultimate aim of public finance.

According to Emperor Yao of the twenty-third century B. C., regarded as a model statesman by the school of Confucius, the aims of the state are of two kinds, economical and ethical. He said: " The virtue of a sovereign is seen in the goodness of the government, and the government is tested by its care for (or nourishing of) the people. There are water, fire, metal, wood, earth, and grain,—these must be duly regulated. There are the rectification of the people's virtue, the promotion of arts and their application in the production of wealth, and the securing and conserving of abundant means of subsistence for the people. These nine services must be harmoniously and systematically developed, so that a myriad generations may perpetually depend on them." [1] It is worthy of note that he considered ethical culture as the most important of the governmental services, although eight out of nine related to the economic welfare of the people. Any constructive program for social development, then, should embrace both the ethical and economic aims.

Conclusions.—Taking into consideration present-day conditions in China, a program of social reconstruction for that country should include the following recommendations: (1) Facilities for elementary and higher education should be greatly increased; (2) adequate roads should be built and several lines of national railways constructed; (3) ship-

[1] *Chinese Classics,* Pt. III, Bk. I, pt. ii, ch. iii, sec. 7, pp. 55-56.

building should be developed and inland and oceanic commerce should be furthered; (4) the disbanded soldiers should be given opportunities for earning their livelihood, and their intra-national migration toward the western and northern less developed or entirely undeveloped territories for permanent settlement should be encouraged and supported by the government; (5) the deepening of river channels, the reclamation of waste lands, and the bettering of drainage and irrigation systems should also be given attention, and modern methods of cultivation and experimentation should be introduced into agriculture, which has been, is, and should always be the main industry of China; (6) the mining industry should be developed, but placed under strict government supervision; (7) a policy of forest conservation should be adopted as early as possible; (8) protective labor legislation should be introduced, and a separate department for the care of the interests of the working population should be created; (9) the public health administration should be greatly extended; (10) the consular service in foreign countries should be improved and extended; (11) the coinage system should be firmly established and such evil practices as the inflation of paper notes and the debasement of token coins should be done away with at any cost; (12) the banking facilities for agricultural, industrial, and commercial development should be encouraged by the central or the provincial governments, and placed under their respective control or supervision; (13) a sound system of central banking and a government treasury should be established, and an amicable relationship should be fostered between public finance and private finance; and (14) last but not least, such educational agencies as institutes for training in public administration or for fiscal research, legislative reference libraries and the like should be developed in order that the reform of fiscal as well as general administration may be accomplished and the quality of legislation may be improved.   In short, China is now facing political, economic and educational problems of the most difficult and most tremendous kind, and for the proper solution of these, both creative and curative measures, both preventive and repressive policies are necessary. But unless fiscal reforms are first achieved, it is difficult to say whether there will be any possibility of solving these problems.

We, the Chinese people, should, however, hold no pessimistic views. We have much to learn from the West in order to enrich our native inheritance; but we are fortunate in that we may deduce many lessons from our ancient philosophers and statesmen. And we may fittingly close our discussion with a few passages from the *Great Learning,* a Confucian text, which comprises the fundamental principles of Chinese political democracy and fiscal ethics. The passages read:

When a ruler loves what the people love, and hates what the people hate, then he is what is called the parent of the people.

Calamities cannot fail to come down upon the one who outrages the natural feeling of men, that is, the one who loves those whom the people hate and hates whom the people love.

Let the producers be many and the non-producers few. Let there be efficiency in production and economy in consumption. This is called a great course for the production of wealth, and it will lead to a constant economic, as well as fiscal, prosperity and sufficiency.

Virtue is the root, and wealth is the result. The former is of primary importance, while the latter is of secondary importance.

Therefore, in a state, pecuniary gain is not to be considered prosperity; but prosperity will be found in social righteousness and fiscal justice.[1]

[1] The *Great Learning* has been used as a primary reader in the elementary schools since the thirteenth century A. D. It is hoped that a more universal and careful study, by the younger generations, of the Confucian principles of fiscal ethics as set forth in this ancient document will help to produce or to cultivate a new and sound citizenship.

APPENDIX I

TABLE OF CHINESE CHRONOLOGY

Stage of Political Development	Name of Epoch	Name of Dynasty or Period [1]	Christian Era
Feudal	Five Emperors [2]	Tai-hao or Pao-hsi Shih	2953–2839 B. C.
		Emperor Yen or Shên-nung Shih [3]	2838–2699 B. C.
		Emperor Huang [3]	2698–2599 B. C.
		Emperor Yao [3]	2357–2256 B. C.
		Emperor Shun [3]	2255–2206 B. C.
	Three Dynasties	Hsia [3]	2205–1766 B. C.
		Yin	1765–1123 B. C.
		Chou (Western)	1122–771 B. C. [4]
	Spring and Autumn and Warring States	Chou (Eastern)	770–247 B. C.

[1] The dynasties whose names are printed in Roman characters ruled the whole empire; those printed in Italics ruled parts of China only. Small kingdoms of no great historical importance are omitted from the table. The kingdom of Wu together with Eastern Tsin, Sung (of the House of Liu), Liang and Chen, are known as the "Six Dynasties."

[2] The period of the rule of the Five Emperors is not definitely known; the dates here given are only conventional.

[3] The different schools of political philosophy in ancient China, excepting the Jurists, all had wise rulers as their model statesmen; namely:

(a) The school of Lao Tzu......Emperor Huang (2698 B. C.).
(b) The school of the Agriculturalists......Emperor Yen or Shên-nung (2838 B. C.).
(c) The school of Mo Ti......Yu the Great, founder of the Hsia dynasty (2205 B. C.).
(d) The school of Confucius......Emperors Yao (2357 B. C.) and Shun (2205 B. C.).

The Jurists believed in progress and held that the system of government of the immediate past should be the model for that of the present; whereas the other schools chose to pattern their systems of government after those of the remote ancient emperors.

[4] According to the *Bamboo Records of Ancient Chinese Chronology*, the Chou dynasty should date from the year 1050 B. C. For a full treatment of the two different systems of Chinese ancient chronology, see Léopold de Saussure, La Chronologie Chinoise Et L'avènement Des Tcheou, *T'oung Pao*, vol. xxiii, No. 5, Paris, 1924, pp. 288 *et sequence*.

APPENDIX I—*Continued*

Stage of Political Development	Name of Epoch	Name of Dynasty or Period	Christian Era
Imperial	Ch'in and Han	Ch'in	221–207 B. C.
		Former or Western Han	206B.C.–6A.D.
		Wang Mang	7–24 A. D.
		Latter or Eastern Han	25–220 A. D.
	Three Kingdoms	*Shu Han*	221–264 A. D.
		Wu	222–280 A. D.
		Wei	220–265 A. D.
	Western and Eastert Tsin	*Tsin* or *Western Tsin*	265–316 A. D.
		Eastern Tsin	317–420 A. D.
	Southern and Northern Dynasties	*Sung* (House of Liu)	420–479 A. D.
		Ch'i	479–502 A. D.
		Liang	502–557 A. D.
		Chen	557–589 A. D.
		Northern Wei	586–534 A. D.
		Eastern Wei	534–550 A. D.
		Northern Ch'i	550–577 A. D.
		Northern Chou	557–581 A. D.
	Sui and T'ang	Sui	581–618 A. D.
		T'ang	618–907 A. D.
	Five Dynasties	*Posterior Liang*	907–923 A. D.
		Posterior T'ang	923–936 A. D.
		Posterior Tsin	936–947 A. D.
		Posterior Han	947–951 A. D.
		Posterior Chou	951–960 A. D.
	Sung, Liao, Kin and Yüan	Sung or Northern Sung (House of Chao)	960–1127 A. D.
		Southern Sung (House of Chao)	1127–1280 A. D.
		Liao	937–1125 A. D.
		Kin	1115–1234 A. D.
		Yüan	1280–1367 A. D.
	Ming and Ts'ing	Ming	1368–1643 A. D.
		Ts'ing	1644–1912 A. D.
Republican	Republican	The Republic	1912 A. D.

APPENDIX II

CURRENCY, WEIGHTS AND MEASURES

Currency

The monetary unit generally used in China is the yuan or Chinese silver dollar, the value of which is approximately $0.50 in United States currency. The Haikwan *tael* is a money of account employed by the Chinese Maritime Customs in collection and statistics. It is uncoined, but has a fixed weight of 583.3 grains of silver 1,000 fine; its value is $1.50 Chinese currency.

A *cash* is legally one-thousandth of a *yuan*.

The National Coinage Act of 1914, provided that the different coins should be as follows:

(a) Silver coins: 1 *yuan* or dollar; 50-*fen* (i. e., a half *yuan* or 50 cents); 20-*fen;* and 10-*fen*.
(b) Nickel coins: 5-*fen*.
(c) Copper coins: 2-*fen;* 1-*fen;* 5-*li* (i. e., *cash*); 2-*li;* 1-*li*.

Weights and Measures

A *catty* is 1-1/3 lbs. or 604.53 grammes.
A *pical* is 133-1/3 lbs. or 60.463 kilogrammes.
A *li* is usually considered 1/3 of an English mile.
A *mou* is 1/6 of an English acre.

In an attempt to unify the system of weights and measures, the Chinese government has taken steps to inaugurate the following standards:

Weights

10 *ssu*	= 1 *hao*.
19 *hao*	= 1 *li*.
10 *li*	= *fen* (candareen).
10 *fen*	= ch'ien (mace.
10 *chien*	= *liang* (tael) = 37.301 grammes.
10 *liang*	= chin (*catty*) = 596.816 grammes.

Capacity

10 *sho*	= 1 *ko*.
10 *ko*	= 1 *sheng*.
10 *sheng*	= 1 *tou* = 10.354688 litres.
5 *tau*	= *hu*.
2 *hu*	= *tan*.

Length

10 *fen*	= 1 *ts'un* (inch).
10 *ts'un*	= 1 *ch'ih* (foot) = .32 metre.
10 *ch'ih*	= 1 *chang* = 3.2 metres.
180 *chang*	= 1 *li* = 576 metres.

BIBLIOGRAPHY

A. Sources in Chinese

I. Confucian Classics:
  a. *The Four Books:*
      The Great Learning.
      The Doctrine of the Mean.
      The Confucian Analects.
      The Works of Mencius.
  b. Other Classics, especially
      Yi King or *Book of Changes.*
      Shee King or *Book of Poetry.*
      Shu King or Book of History.
      Chou Kuan or *The Constitution of the Chou Dynasty.*
      Li Ki or *Record of Rites.*
      Ch'un Ch'iu or *Spring and Autumn,* with the
      Commentaries of Tso, Kung-yang, and Ku-liang.

II. The Nine Historical Researches, especially

  Tu Yu's *History of Political Institutes.*
  Ma Tuan-lin's *General Researches on Political Institutions and
      Literary Authorities.*
  Continuation of Ma Tuan-lin's General Research.
  The Political Institutes of the Ts'ing Dynasty.

III. The Twenty-Two Ancient Philosophers, especially

  The Works of Lao Tzŭ with Yen Fuh's Commentaries.
  The Works of Chuang Tzŭ with Kao Ching-fan's Commentaries.
  The Works of Kuan Tzŭ with Fang Yuen-lin's Commentaries.
  The Works of Mo Ti with Sun I-jang's Collected Commentaries.

IV. The Twenty-Four Dynastic Histories, especially

  The Historical Record.
  The History of the Former Han Dynasty.
  The History of the Latter Han Dynasty.
  The Old History of the T'ang Dynasty.
  The New History of the T'ang Dynasty.
  The History of the Sung Dynasty.
  The History of the Yüan Dynasty.
  The History of the Ming Dynasty.

200

V. The Works of Modern Writers.

Chang, Car Sun, *Memorandum on the National Constitution,* Shanghai, 1923.

Chia, S. Y., *The Fiscal History of the Republic of China,* 2 vols., Shanghai, 1917.

Chou, Pao-luan, *History of Chinese Banking,* Shanghai, 1919.

Fêng, Sun-chan, *Chapters on Chinese Fiscal History,* Peking, 1911.

Hsü, Chang-shui, *History of Chinese Domestic Public Debts,* Shanghai, 1923.

Hu, Chun, *Chinese Fiscal History,* Shanghai, 1919.

Hu, Suh, *An Outline of the History of Chinese Philosophy,* vol. 1, Shanghai, 1918.

——, *The Works of Hu Suh,* 3 vols., Shanghai, 1925.

Kuo, Chung-hsiew, *A History of the Provisional Government of the Republic of China,* Shanghai, 1917.

Li, Y. C., *Li Wei-kung the Statesman,* 2nd ed., Shanghai, 1911.

Liang, Chi-ch'ao, *Wang An-shih the Statesman,* 3rd ed., Shanghai, 1911.

——, *Kuan Tzŭ the Statesman,* 3rd ed., Shanghai, 1911.

——, " On the Causes of the Neglect of Fiscal Study in China," *Ta Chun Hua Monthly,* Feb. 1914, Shanghai.

——, *Development of Political Thought in Ancient China,* Shanghai, 1923.

Ma, Y. C., *Lectures on Current Economic Problems in China,* 3 vols., Shanghai and Peking, 1922-1926.

Sheng, T., *Studies in Chinese Customs Administration,* Ministry of Finance, Bureau of Markets, Shanghai, 1919.

Sun, Yat-sen, Two Addresses: one on the *Three Fundamental Democratic Principles* and the other on the *Five-Power Constitution,* Canton, 1921.

Wang, C. S., *The Likin Problem in China,* Shanghai, 1917.

Yen, Tsai-chih, *Land Taxation in China: An account of the existing system with some recommendations for its reform,* Peking, 1915.

——, *China's Fiscal Problem Series—Taxation,* two vols., Peking, 1922.

——, *China's Fiscal Problem Series—Public Indebtedness,* Peking, 1923.

VI. Official Documents, Pamphlets, and Other Publications.

Classified Laws and Ordinances of the Republic of China, published by the Ministry of Justice, Peking.

The Fiscal Reports of the Twenty-two Provinces of the Year 1909, published by the Ministry of Finance, Peking.

The Kiang-su Association Series: Shanghai, 1921-22.
   Vol. I. Provincial Constitution
   Vol. II. Local Self-government.
   Vol. III. Public Finance.
The China Year Book, 1924-5, Shanghai.
The Chinese Bankers Weekly, Shanghai.
The Chinese Bankers Monthly, Peking.
The Eastern Miscellany, Shanghai.
The Journal of Political Science, Peking.
The Justice, Shanghai.
The Pacific Monthly, Shanghai.
The Past Fifty Years, The Shun Pao, Shanghai, China, 1923.
The Publications of the Association for Chinese Classical Research, Shanghai.
The Quarterly of Chinese Classical Research, National University of Peking, Peking.

B. Sources in Languages Other than Chinese

Adams, H. C., *Science of Finance,* New York, 1909.
——, *Public Debts,* New York, 1887.
American Relations with China. Report of the Conference held at Johns Hopkins University, September 17-20, 1925.
American Political Science Review, The, Baltimore.
American Economic Review, The, Evanston, Illinois.
Annals of the American Academy of Political and Social Science, The, Philadelphia.
Arnold, Julean, *Commercial Handbook of China,* Washington, D. C., Vol. 1, 1919; Vol. 2, 1920.
Barnes, H. E., *Sociology and Political Theory,* New York, 1924.
Bastable, C. F., *Public Finance,* 3rd ed., London, 1903.
Bau, M. J., *Modern Democracy in China,* Shanghai, 1924.
——, *The Foreign Relations of China: A History and a Survey,* New York, 1922.
Bentham, Jeremy, *An Introduction to the Principles of Morals and Legislation,* Oxford Ed., 1907.
Bolles, Albert Sidney, *American Finance, with chapters on Money and Banking,* New York, 1901.
British Chamber of Commerce Journal, The, Shanghai.
Brown, H. G., *The Economics of Taxation,* New York, 1924.
Brunnert, H., and Hagelstrom, V., *Present-Day Political Organization of China* (Translated by A. Beltchenko and E. E. Moran), Shanghai, 1910.
Bryce, James, *Modern Democracies,* 2 vols., London, 1921.
Bulletin of the National Tax Association, The, Lancaster, Pa.
Bullock, C. J., *Selected Readings in Public Finance,* 3rd ed., New York, 1924.

Bureau of Municipal Research, *A Handbook of Municipal Accounting,* New York, 1914.

Butler, Nicholas Murray, *The Faith of a Liberal; Essays and Addresses on Political Principles and Public Policies,* New York, 1924.

Cannan, Edwin, *History of Local Rates in Relation to the Proper Distribution of the Burden of Taxation,* 2nd ed., London, 1912.

Carter, T. F., *The Invention of Printing in China and its Spread Westward,* New York, 1925.

Carus, Paul, *Lao-Tze's Tao-Teh-King,* Chinese-English, with introduction, translation, and notes, Chicago, 1898.

Chand, Gyan, *The Financial System of India,* London, 1926.

Chang, Ying-Hua, *The Financial Reconstruction of China,* Peking, 1923.

Chen, S. K., *The System of Taxation in China, 1614-1911, Columbia Univ. Studies,* Vol. LIX, No. 2.

Chen, H. C., *The Economic Principles of Confucius and His School, Columbia Univ. Studies,* Vols. XLIV, XLV, New York, 1911.

Cheng, Sih-Gung, *Modern China, a Political Study,* Oxford, 1919.

Chang, S. C., *Chinese Politics and Professionalism,* Shanghai, 1922.

"China's Finances: A Summary," *Chinese Economic Monthly,* Nov. 1925.

China Weekly Review, Shanghai.

The China Year Book, edited by G. W. Woodhead, Tientsin, 1925.

The Chinese Classics, translated by James Legge, 7 vols., London, 1865-1895.

Chinese Economic Monthly, Peking.

Chinese Maritime Customs, Treaties and Conventions between China and the Foreign Nations, Shanghai, 1908-1925.

Chinese Political and Social Science Review, Peking.

Chu, C., *The Tariff Problem in China, Columbia Univ. Studies,* Vol. XXII, New York, Nov. 2, 1916.

"*Chuang Tse, Mystic, Moralist, and Social Reformer,*" A Translation of Chuang Tse's works by H. A. Giles, London, 1889.

Clark, J. M., *Social Control of Business,* Chicago, 1926.

Comparative Statement of China's Finances, 1912-1923: Figures showing public debt, income and expenditure, with summarized tables. *British Chamber of Commerce Journal,* Feb. 1925, Shanghai.

Cordier, Henri, *Histoire Generale de la Chine,* 4 vols., Paris, 1920.

Culbertson, William Smith, *International Economic Policies: A Survey of the Economics of Diplomacy,* New York, 1925.

Cohn, Gustav, *The Science of Finance,* translated by T. B. Veblen, Chicago, 1895.

Current History, New York.

Dalton, Hugh, *Principles of Public Finance,* New York, 1923.

Daniels, W. M., *The Elements of Public Finance,* New York, 1911.

Dewey, Davis Rich, *Financial History of the United States,* 9th ed., New York, 1924.

Dewey, John, *Social Institution and the Study of Morals.* Syllabus, Columbia University, 1923.

——, "What Outlawry of War is Not," *The New Republic,* October 3, 1923.

Economic Journal, The, London.

Economica, London.

Edkins, Joseph, *Chinese Currency,* Shanghai, 1901.

——, *Banking and Prices in China,* Shanghai, 1905.

——, *The Revenue and Taxation of the Chinese Empire,* Shanghai, 1903.

Fetter, Frank A., *Modern Economic Problems,* 2nd ed., New York, 1922.

Finanz-Archiv: Zeitschrift für das gesamte Finanzwesen, Stuttgart und Berlin.

Fiske, J., *American Political Ideals,* Boston, 1911.

Fung, Yu-lan, *A Comparative Study of Life Ideals,* Shanghai, 1924.

Foreign Policy Association, *The Conflict of Policies in China: Extraterritoriality, customs autonomy, treaty revision,* P. W. Kuo & C. C. Batchelder, New York, 1925.

Gettell, R. G., *History of Political Thought,* New York, 1924.

Goodnow, F. J., *China: An Analysis,* Baltimore, 1926.

Gregory, T. E. G., *Tariffs: A Study in Method,* London, 1921.

Groseclose, E. E., "Chinese Revenues for 1925," *Commercial Reports, No. 15,* April 19, 1926, U. S. Dept. of Commerce.

Grice, J. Watson, *National and Local Finance,* London, 1910.

Gulick, L. H., "A Model System of Municipal Revenues," *Bulletins of the National Tax Association,* vol. VI, 1920-1921.

Gutzlaff, C., *China Opened,* 2 vols.. London, 1838.

Haig, Robert M., "The American System of Special Assessments and its Applicability to Other Countries." Paper presented before the Second Pan-American Scientific Congress, Washington, Dec. 27, 1915-Jan. 8, 1916. Washington Govt. Printing Office, 1917.

——, *The Exemption of Improvements from Taxation in Canada and the United States,* New York, 1915.

——, *The Taxation of Excess Profits in Great Britain,* American Economic Association, 1920.

Hamilton, Alexander, *The Works of Alexander Hamilton,* Henry C. Lodge's edition, New York, 1904.

Hart, Sir Robert, *Memorandum on Land Tax Reform,* Chinese Maritime Customs Service, Special Series, 1904.

Hayes, Carlton J. H., *Essays on Nationalism,* New York, 1926.

Herslet, G. E. P., and Parkes, E., *Treaties, etc. between Great Britain and China; and between China and Foreign Powers,* 2 vols., London, 1908.

Higgs, H., *The Financial System of the United Kingdom,* London, 1914.

Hobhouse, L. T., *Liberalism,* London, 1911.

Hobson, John A., *Democracy After the War*, 4th ed., New York, 1919.

——, *Free Thought in the Social Sciences*, London, 1926.

——, *Taxation in the New State*, New York, 1920.

Hodges, C., " China Shackled by Treaty Powers," *Current History*, April 1926, New York.

Hollander, Jacob H., *American Citizenship and Economic Welfare*, Baltimore, 1919.

——, *Economic Liberalism*, New York, 1925.

Hornbeck, Stanley K., *Contemporary Politics in the Far East*, New York, 1916.

Hsia, Ching-lin, *Studies in Chinese Diplomatic History*, Shanghai, 1925.

Hsieh, P. C., *The Government of China* (1614-1911), Baltimore, 1925.

Hsu, Chih, *Railway Problems in China, Columbia Univ. Studies*, Vol. LXVI, No. 2, New York, 1915.

Hu, Suh, *The Development of the Logical Method in Ancient China*, Shanghai, 1922.

Huang, F. H., *Public Debts in China, Columbia Univ. Studies*, Vol. LXXXV, No. 2, New York, 1918.

Huang, L. H., *The Land Tax in China, Columbia Univ. Studies*, Vol. LXXX, No. 3, New York, 1918.

Hunter, M. H., *Outlines of Public Finance*, New York, 1921.

Jamieson, Sir George, " The Revenue and Expenditure of the Chinese Empire," *British Diplomatic and Consular Reports*, Miscellaneous Series, No. 415, 1897.

Jensen, Jens Peter, *Problems of Public Finance*, New York, 1924.

Jones, R., *The Nature and First Principle of Taxation*, London, 1914.

Journal of Land and Public Utility Economics, The, Chicago.

Journal of Political Economy, The, Chicago.

Judson, H. P., *Our Federal Republic*, New York, 1925.

Laski, Harold J., *A Grammar of Politics*, London, 1925.

" List of Chinese Internal Loans outstanding on Jan. 1, 1926." E. Kann, *British Chamber of Commerce Journal*, Shanghai, Jan. 1926.

Koo, V. K. W., *The Status of Aliens in China, Columbia Univ. Studies*, Vol. I, No. 2, New York, 1912.

Kuo Min Tang Students League, *Program for the Reconstruction of China*, New York, 1925.

Kuo, P. W., and Count Michimasa Soyeshima, *Oriental Interpretations of the Far East Problem*, Chicago, 1925.

Kwang, Eu-Yang, *The Political Reconstruction of China, St. John's University Studies*, No. 1, Shanghai, 1921.

League of Nations, *Memorandum on Public Finance*, Geneva, 1921.

——, *Report on Double Taxation Submitted to the Financial Committee, by Professors Bruins, Einaudi, Seligman, and Sir Josiah Stamp*, Geneva, 1923.

League of Nations, *Reports on Double Taxation and Fiscal Evasion, by the Government Experts,* Geneva, 1924-1925.

Lee, F. E., "The Significance of Foreign Financial Control in China," *Annals of American Academy of Political and Social Science,* Nov. 1925.

——, *Currency, Banking and Finance in China, Trade Promotion Series,* No. 27, 1926. Washington Govt. Printing Office.

Lee, Mabel P., *The Economic History of China: A Study in Soil Exhaustion, Columbia Univ. Studies,* Vol. XCIX, No. 1, New York, 1921.

Leong, Y. K., and Tao, L. K., *Village and Town Life in China,* London, 1925.

Leroy-Beaulieu, Paul, *Traité de la Science des finances,* 8th ed., Paris, 1912.

Li, C. S., *Central and Local Finance in China, Columbia Univ. Studies,* Vol. XCIX, No. 2, New York, 1921.

Li Ki or *Book of Rites,* translated by Legge in the "Sacred Book of the East Series," London.

Lindahl, E., *Die Gerechtigkeit der Besteuerung,* Lund, 1919.

Liu, Ting Mien, *Modern Tariff Policies with Special Reference to China,* Peking, 1925.

Lovett, R. M., "Siamese Precedent for China; Extraterritoriality and Tariff Autonomy," *The New Republic,* Mar. 31, 1926, New York.

Lowell, A. Lawrence, *Greater European Governments,* rev. ed., Cambridge, 1925.

Lutz, H. L., *Public Finance,* New York, 1924.

MacNair, Harley Farnsworth, *Modern Chinese History: Selected Readings,* Shanghai, 1923.

MacMurray, J. V. A., *Treaties and Agreements with and Concerning China, 1894-1919,* New York, 1921.

Marx, Karl, *Zur Kritik der Politischen Oekonomie,* Berlin, 1859.

Mellon, A. W., *Taxation: The People's Business,* New York, 1924.

Merriam, C. E., *New Aspects of Politics,* Chicago, 1925.

Mill, J. S., *Considerations on Representative Government,* New York, 1905.

——, *Principles of Political Economy, with Some of Their Application to Social Philosophy,* edited by Sir W. J. Ashley, London, 1920.

Millard, Thomas F., *Democracy and the Eastern Question,* New York, 1919.

——, "Taxation Causes Chinese Unrest," *The New York Times,* April 4, 1926.

Mo Ti des sozial-ethikers und seiner Schüler philosophische Werke, translated by Alfred Forke, Berlin, 1922.

Montesquieu, Charles de Secondat, *The Spirit of Laws,* translated by Thomas Nugent, 2 vols., New York, 1873.

Munro, W. B., *The Governments of Europe,* New York, 1925.
——, *Municipal Government and Administration,* New York, 1923.
Morse, Hosea Ballou, *The Gilds of China,* London, 1909.
——, *The Trade and Administration of China,* London, 1920.
——, "Chinese Currency," *Journal of the Royal Asiatic Society, North China Branch,* 1907, vol. 38.
Otte, F., "Notes on the Chinese Native Customs System," *Chinese Economic Monthly,* Feb. 1926.
Overlach, Theodore Williams, *Foreign Financial Control in China,* New York, 1919.
Padoux, G., *Consolidation of China's Unsecured Debts: A Survey of the Country's Financial Problems,* Peking, 1925.
Page, Thomas Walker, *Making the Tariff in the United States,* New York, 1924.
Peck, Harvey W., *Taxation and Welfare,* New York, 1925.
Peel, Colonel Sidney, "Distinctions between Central and Local Finance in England and China," *The Chinese Social and Political Science Review,* April, 1926.
The Peking Leader, Special Customs Conference Edition, Peking, October 26, 1925.
Plehn, Carl C., *Introduction to Public Finance,* 4th ed., New York, 1920.
Pigou, A. C., *The Economics of Welfare,* 2nd ed., London, 1924.
Political Science Quarterly, New York.
Pott, William S. A., *Chinese Political Philosophy,* New York, 1925.
Proceedings of the National Tax Association, Lancaster, Pa.
Quarterly Journal of Economics, The, Cambridge, Mass.
Remer, C. F., *Readings in Economics for China,* Shanghai, 1922.
Revue de science et de législation financières, Paris.
Revue économique internationale, Paris.
Rich, Raymond T., *Extraterritoriality and Tariff Autonomy in China, International Understanding Series,* Shanghai, 1925.
Rignano, Eugenio, *The Social Significance of the Inheritance Tax,* translated and adapted by W. J. Shultz, New York, 1924.
Roscher, W., *System des Finanzwissenschaft,* Stuttgart, 1901.
Ruskin, John, *Unto This Last,* Four Essays on the First Principles of Political Economy, New York, 1866.
Russell, Bertrand, *Political Ideals,* New York, 1917.
——, *The Problem of China,* New York, 1922.
Seager, Henry R., *Practical Problems in Economics,* New York, 1923.
Seligman, E. R. A., *The Economic Interpretation of History,* New York, 1907.
——, *Essays in Taxation,* 10th ed., New York, 1925.
——, *The Income Tax,* New York, 1914.
——, *Progressive Taxation in Theory and Practice,* 2nd ed., American Economic Association, 1908.

Seligman, E. R. A., *The Shifting and Incidence of Taxation*, 4th ed., New York, 1921.

——, *Studies in Public Finance*, New York, 1925.

Shirras, G. Findlay, *The Science of Public Finance*, 2nd ed., London, 1925.

Short, Lloyd Milton, *The Development of National Administrative Organization in the United States*, Washington, D. C., 1923.

Simcox, Edith J., *Primitive Civilizations*, vol. 2, New York, 1894.

Smith, Adam, *Wealth of Nations*, ed. by Edwin Cannan, London, 1904.

Smith, James Haldane, *Collectivist Economics*, London, 1925.

——, *Economic Moralism: An Essay in Constructive Economics*, London, 1916.

Snowden, Philip, *Labor and National Finance*, London, 1920.

Stamp, Sir J., *The Fundamental Principles of Taxation in the Light of Modern Developments*, London, 1921.

——, *Studies in Current Problems in Finance and Government*, London, 1924.

——, *Wealth and Taxable Capacity*, London, 1922.

Sun Yat-sen, *The International Development of China*, New York, 1922.

Suzuki, Daisetz Teiters, *A Brief History of Early Chinese Philosophy*, London, 1914.

Sze, S. K. Alfred, Chinese Minister to the United States, *Addresses*, Baltimore, 1926.

Sze, T. Y., *China and the Most-Favored-Nation Clause*, New York, 1925.

Taoist Teaching in the Book of Lieh Tse, translated by Lionel Giles, in the "Wisdom of the East Series," London, 1912.

Tang, L. L., and M. S. Miller, "Political Aspect of International Finance in Russia and China," *Economica*, March 1925, London.

Taussig, F. W., *The Tariff History of the United States*, New York, 1923.

Tazaki, Masayoshi, *A Study of Yu-Kung* (or the Tribute System of Yü) (in Japanese), Tokio, 1920.

Le Tcheou-li, or *Rites des Tscheou*, translated by E. Biot, 2 vols., Paris, 1851.

Tugwell, R. G., and others, *The Trend of Economics*, New York, 1924.

Vinacke, H. M., *Modern Constitutional Development in China*, Princeton, 1920.

Vissering, W., *On Chinese Currency*, Leiden, 1877.

Wagel, Srinivas R., *Finance in China*, Shanghai, 1914.

Wagner, Adolf, *Finanzwissenschaft*, Leipzig, 1889.

Watkins, G. P., *Welfare as an Economic Quantity*, Boston, 1915.

Weale, Putnam, *The Fight for the Republic of China*, New York, 1917.

Webb, Sidney, *Grants in Aid: A Criticism and a Proposal*, London, 1920.

——, "What about the Rates?" or "Municipal Finance and Municipal Autonomy," *Fabian Tracts*, No. 172, London, July 1913.

Weber, G. A., *Organized Efforts for the Improvement of Methods of Administration in the United Staes*, Washington, 1919.

Wei, T. S., "Chinese Banks Should Hold the Customs Deposits," *China Weekly Review,* Special Customs Conference Ed., Nov. 1, 1925.

Wei, W. P., *The Currency Problem in China, Columbia Univ. Studies,* Vol. LIX, No. 3, New York, 1914.

Werner, E. T. C., *Descriptive Sociology,* No. 9 (Chinese), London, 1910.

Weston, Stephen F., *Principles of Justice in Taxation, Columbia Univ. Studies,* Vol. XVI, No. 2, New York, 1903.

Williams, E. T., *China Yesterday and Today,* New York, 1923.

Willoughby, W. F., "Memorandum on Reform of Land Tax System in China," Vol. II, Nos. 1 and 2, *Chinese Political and Social Science Review.*

——, *The Problem of a National Budget,* New York, 1918.

——, Willoughby, W. W., and S. M. Lindsay, *The System of Financial Administration of Great Britain,* Washington, 1917.

Willoughby, W. W., *Foreign Rights and Interests in China,* Baltimore, 1920.

——, *China at the Conference: A Report,* Baltimore, 1922.

——, *Constitutional Government in China, Present Conditions and Prospects,* Washington, 1922.

Wright, Q., and Quigley, H. S., "Progress of Peking Tariff Conference," *Current History,* January 1926.

Winston, A. P., "Chinese Finance under the Republic," *Quarterly Journal of Economics,* Cambridge, Mass., August 1916.

Yen, Hawkling L., *A Survey of Constitutional Development in China, Columbia Univ. Studies,* Vol. XI, No. 1, New York, 1911.

Yi King or *Book of Changes,* translated by James Legge in the "Sacred Book of the East Series," London, 1882.

INDEX

211